BEFORE AND AFTER THE FIRST EARTH DAY, 1970

A history of environmentalism,
its success, failures, errors,
and why climate change is the wrong issue
for today

by David M. Guion

Chapter 1 Before Earth Day

Earth Day takes place every year on April 22. The United States has observed Earth Day every year beginning in 1970. Earth Day has been observed internationally since 1990. Why? What difference does it make?

To answer the first question requires looking at the state of the environment since the end of the Second World War, how environmental questions first came to the attention of the American public, and how new tactics redefined environmental law. To answer the second requires understanding both how many environmental problems of the 1960s have been solved, how many remain unsolved, what new ones have surfaced since then. Along the way, clearly the environmental movement accomplished some wonderful work, but its leaders did not do everything right. Environmental issues united the country in 1970, but they have become divisive, largely because environmentalists today have kept insisting on the worst errors for nearly half a century.

Except for the attack on Pearl Harbor, the Second World War took place entirely in Europe, Asia, and Africa. The United States suffered rationing and considerable loss of life, but since the fighting did not take place here, its infrastructure and manufacturing capacity remained unscathed. All other economies were in ruins.

In the 16 years between the start of the Great Depression and the end of the war, Americans had to deal with scarcity. At first, with high unemployment, people could not afford to buy many goods and services. Manufacturers tailored their production to satisfy demand that was lower than in the prosperity of the 1920s. With America's entry into the war, factories began to manufacture materials necessary for the war effort, even if they were completely unrelated to the companies' core businesses. As the war brought the country out of Depression, people could still not buy many consumer goods. Manufacturers were not making them, and the government rationed many different materials.

When the war was over, Americans could spend without restraint, and manufacturers churned out products old and new to satisfy the pent-up demand. They did not know when to stop. Factories produced more than Americans could buy. Exporting goods could not be an option until economies destroyed by the war began to recover. For the first time in history, a society faced a crisis not of scarcity, but overabundance.

Unfortunately, the solution the nation's leaders found required American families to give up frugality and become prodigally wasteful. The Roosevelt administration responded to wartime conditions by appealing to traditional American frugality. It rationed basic materials from steel to sugar to make them available for the military. In stark contrast, the Bush administration responded to the attack on 9/11 by urging Americans to go shopping. By that time, practicing frugality and sacrifice would have destroyed the nation's entire economic structure. Bush was hardly the first President to offer spending as a solution to a national crisis. Every administration since Eisenhower's has had to issue the same call. Most of the American population alive today cannot remember when frugality characterized our society.

A curious juxtaposition of events took place in the early 1960s. In 1961, Sam Yorty successfully campaigned for mayor of Los Angeles promising to eliminate the requirement that citizens separate their garbage. Soon wet garbage, trash, and paper mingled together in the same dump, making the modern landfill necessary. The following year, Rachel Carson published *Silent Spring,* drawing public attention to the state of the environment for the first time. Yorty, considered one of the worst big-city mayors of the post-war era, has been largely forgotten, but destroying the habit of separating trash has been an unmitigated environmental disaster. Carson galvanized the environmental movement, and her books remain best sellers.

The post-war boom, the new economics, and the American character

Throughout most of history and most of the world, people have struggled with the scarcity of food and other materials. In the prosperity that began after the Second World War, America struggled with a new problem. Efficiency and automation led to unprecedented productivity, but how were companies supposed to sell everything they made? Factories churned out not only necessities, but frills and luxuries. Then they had to figure out how to sell this glut. Vance Packard described the radical changes that took place in American society in at least three books. Much of the material in this section comes from *The Waste Makers* (1960).

By 1960, the average American consumed twice as many goods as before the war. A high percentage of what people owned was not essential for survival. Even people struggling with inadequate housing, food, and clothing managed to have radios, televisions, and other luxuries. Except they did not seem like luxuries. Marketers had learned to make nearly everything seem like essential necessities.

Factories became more and more efficient and productive. By 1960, fifteen years after the war ended, the amount of goods a single worker could produce in a given amount of time grew by about 3% annually. Automation in the form of machinery doing tasks previously done by craftsmen added greatly to the growth in productivity.

The vast majority of American homes had at least one each of refrigerator, stove, and television. Most families also had vacuum cleaners, sewing machines, electric toasters and mixers, and many other similar appliances. Passenger cars outnumbered families. Manufacturers had to contend with the problem of how to sell when most families already owned their product. They could sell replacements by making products that broke down more readily than older ones. They could induce consumers to buy more than one of each item. They could introduce technological improvements, or at least noticeable changes, to make what people already owned obsolete. They did all that and more. Consider: once upon a time, not all that long ago,

- If an umbrella, pen, clock, or other common item broke; owners took it somewhere to get it fixed.
- When a man's razor got dull, he replaced the blade instead of throwing out the whole razor. Actually, before that, my grandfather and lots of other men still used straight razors and sharpened them with a strop.
- When a pen ran out of ink, people put in a refill. They did not discard the whole pen. Many people actually still used fountain pens
- Parents of babies either laundered cloth diapers themselves or used a diaper service. Disposable diapers might be much easier to put on, but they're still every bit as nasty to change. And they take up lots of space in our landfills.
- Paper plates and plastic "silverware" were used only at picnics and cookouts. Never for ordinary meals at home
- Water came from the tap. People poured it into a glass, which then got washed. If they were away from home, they drank from a water fountain. If they went for a walk or something and wanted to take water, they put it in a canteen

Milk and soft drinks used to come in glass bottles. We paid a deposit and returned them to the store when they were empty in order to get the deposit back.

Along side genuine technological improvements in products, manufacturers relied on gimmicks like the annual new car competition to see which model sported the flashiest fins. The 1960s introduced lava lamps, mood rings, black lights, platform shoes, love beads, slot cars, hula hoops, eight-track players, and pet rocks. Numerous companies owned multiple brands of the same product, such as dishwashing detergent, in a bid to increase their share of shelf space in the stores.

The federal government's leadership in waste

The federal government encouraged overproduction in agriculture. It spent billions of dollars every year enabling farmers to grow much more food than Americans could eat. Then it spent more millions of dollars on metal to build storage bins to keep it all. New agricultural technology starting in the 1930s had greatly increased agricultural yields, the beginning of the so-called green revolution. Healthier plants required more water and fertilizer. Manure would have been the best fertilizer, but fertilizer made from petroleum was less expensive and had the advantage of an industrial marketing campaign behind it. Farmers poured truckloads of synthetic fertilizer into fields that should have been allowed to lay fallow.

Defense spending amounted to 10% of the total output of goods and services. The stock market went into a tailspin at any hint of a reduction in defense spending. Politicians could hardly advocate cutting back on it. Their rhetoric pointed to the Russian threat, but in fact, any reduction in the arms industry would put some of their constituents out of work. The military gladly paid hundreds of dollars for parts available in stores for pocket change. If anything needed painting, the services ordered more paint than necessary for the project and put the surplus in a warehouse, where no one would ever look when more paint of the same color was wanted.

The whole concept of economic growth started in the postwar years. Both Democrats and Republicans called for more growth. They only had different ideas on how to achieve it. Again, everyone gave the supposedly rapid growth of the Soviet Union as the reason why the U.S. needed to grow, despite the fact, acknowledged by as least some economists, that Russia, with only about 5% of American production of consumer goods, had no chance of catching up with the American economy even if it was growing a little faster.

No one in positions of political power and influence attempted to explain how production of pinball machines or cleaners designed to clean only one thing—windows or floors or countertops, etc., but not anything else--would add to our military preparedness. No one attempted to distinguish between desirable or undesirable growth. No one questioned that it was a good idea to put up thousands of houses on prime farmland. Everyone assumed that growth, any growth, was inherently a good thing.

Three postwar recessions before 1960, the last being the most serious, were directly caused by the fact that American factories churned out more products than the American people could consume. No one stopped to consider that abundance itself was the problem. Inventory in warehouses was something bad for the economy in every industry except agriculture.

Rather than reduce production to the level of reasonable consumption, manufacturers, economists, and politicians pushed the concept of consumerism, the idea that the public must consume factory output as quickly as factories could produce it. Advertisers had to work very hard to stimulate desire and induce people to expand their conception of what they needed and wanted. At every economic crisis, "experts" began to declare solemnly that consumers were not spending enough.

Such a high level of consumption demanded strategies to promote wastefulness. Several emerged. Disposable drinking cups, napkins, razors, pens, and other goods ensured that people would buy them over and over again rather than continue to use and care for what they had. It became harder and harder to get anything repaired, because factories and stores made it cheaper to buy a new umbrella, for example, and nudged repairmen out of business. Companies planned for introducing technological improvements (real and substantial or otherwise) in such a way that what people already owned would become, or at least appear, obsolete.

This system has resulted in a higher level of physical wellbeing and mobility than the world has ever known. Even the poorest Americans in the 1960s had vast wealth compared to all but the most affluent people in the so-called Third World. Even Americans who remained anxious about finding their next meal very likely owned some frills and luxury items. It is certainly a good thing that the poor were no longer living on the verge of starvation, but every economic and political system has shortcomings. Every one of them has undesirable consequences. One of ours happens to be an economy that appears to depend on wastefulness that puts such a strain on the environment.

The popularity of automobiles has led to massive highway construction and urban sprawl. Think of how much land we have sacrificed in the process. Even cities with good public transportation have rings of suburbs that lack both good public transportation and neighborhoods with stores or other amenities within walking distance. Construction of expressways and bypasses cannot keep up with increased traffic and therefore cannot prevent traffic jams and longer commute times.

Waste mismanagement

By 1960 the average American family tossed 750 metal cans every year. Everyone, man, woman, and child, annually accounted for 18 tons of trash. The American lifestyle required ten times as much raw material as anyone else in the world, not counting food, but someone who forgot something on a shopping trip likely did not think twice about getting in the car and going back for it.

Already, Americans consumed more raw materials than the land could produce. The nation had become dependent on imports for a growing number of resources, especially metals and petroleum. Demand for wood, paper, and water had begun to outstrip nature's ability to provide them. Meanwhile consumerism had produced serious water pollution both in the production and use of goods. Tap water in some places actually had suds. Plastics had begun to reach sufficient quality to replace metals and woods for many applications, but whatever pressure plastic took from those resources added to the overuse of oil, its basic raw material.

Theoretically, salvaging scrap from trash, including junked cars, could reduce dependence on virgin material, but it was not economical. Huge piles of junked cars dotted the landscape. I remember in childhood pointing out the land of broken cars. I find in researching this book that salvage operations could barely make a profit, because steel companies had developed new manufacturing techniques that reduced their use of scrap.

As the nation produced more and more trash, it had to find a way to deal with it. Advertising for consumer goods emphasized how much more convenient they were and how much time and effort they saved. Americans came to expect the same convenience with everything they no longer wanted. As a child growing up in the late 1950s, I remember my mother carefully wrapping the garbage (food wastes) in newspapers every night and putting them in a smelly garbage can by the garage. A company emptied it every week. We put trash (bottles, cans, excess wire coat hangers, broken toys, and the like) in a different can by the garage, and a different company hauled it off. We did not throw out pop bottles; we had to pay a deposit on them, so we returned the empties to the store. As for waste paper, it was my job to empty the wastebaskets from time to time into an incinerator and watch over it while it burned.

I suppose that was common practice all over the country. It certainly was in Los Angeles. Before 1961, Los Angeles had a complicated system of waste management, in part because of its reputation of having the dirtiest air in the country. It included source separation, recycling, and backyard trash incineration. Source separation simply means that citizens had to separate organic wastes (food and other garbage) from other trash, just as my hometown did. Trucks collected garbage on one day and noncombustible trash on another and delivered them either to open dumps or incinerators. Because of material shortages during the Second World War, an active market existed for scrap metal, newspapers, and glass. The primary discussion of air pollution comes later in this chapter, but in 1955 the County Board of Supervisors passed an ordinance that limited backyard incineration to specific hours of the day. It finally banned the practice entirely. As a result, households had to deal with three collections: garbage, noncombustible trash, and combustible trash.

Charges of mismanagement, poor service, and corruption started to plague the system in the 1950s. It became the primary issue in the 1961 campaign for mayor between incumbent Norris Poulson and successful challenger Sam Yorty. Yorty's populist campaign railed against the "elites" who were connected to organized crime and stood in the way of efficiency. He expressed profound pity for the inconvenience to the poor housewives of Los Angeles caused by the current system and promised to eliminate source separation. His solution, already being pursued by both city and county sanitation departments, was the sanitary landfill. He claimed that a single collection would save the city money, as well as make life easier for housewives. Los Angeles had plenty of canyons, land that seemed to have no better use than to receive garbage. Proponents of landfills promised that when the sites reached capacity, they could be converted to usable land for golf courses, botanical gardens, or even housing.

Objections to the landfills began by the mid-1970s. It turns out that "sanitary" landfills released methane, which besides posing an explosion hazard, added to the city's air quality woes. They also leached a potent stew of chemicals that contaminated groundwater. It had not occurred to anyone that hazardous wastes require special treatment. Landfills are inherently a crazy and dangerous chemistry experiment to see what happens when a variety of acid wastes met a variety of alkaline wastes among all the other substances thrown together in one place. Additionally, conservationists fought to protect the Santa Monica Mountains from development. The issue that Yorty rode to power turned out to be his undoing, and he eventually lost to Tom Bradley.

I have no personal recollection of Yorty; I grew up in Ohio. Somehow, though, mingling compostable garbage with at least partly recyclable solid waste into one unmanageable mishmash became the national norm. At some point, my hometown also banned backyard incineration. I recall how strange it felt to mingle waste paper, cans, and food waste in the same trashcan. Sanitary landfills, which seemed like the cheapest and safest method of waste disposal in the early 1960s soon proved otherwise, not only in Los Angeles, but nationwide.

Ironically, the environmental movement as we know it today began before the end of the decade. Recycling programs to replace the ones scrapped in the postwar prosperity came only later. A 1969 "survival walk" from Modesto, California to Sacramento resulted in a new drop-off recycling center each day of the march. Nationwide, 3,000 drop-off centers were established in 1970 as part of Earth Day activities. Curbside collection programs came only later. By that time, perhaps older people recalled recycling and conservation as Depression and wartime necessities and resisted doing it again. Certainly younger people, having recently been freed from the necessity of separating garbage, did not want to have to do it again.

The practice of recycling would probably have caught on faster than it did if everyone had still been in the habit of discarding wet and dry garbage into different collection receptacles. If the practice of separation had continued, it would have been possible to compost the wet garbage. As it is, the commingling of wet and dry garbage limits waste disposal options. In the U.S., most waste eventually winds up in landfills.

I firmly believe that if Americans had had an uninterrupted practice of separating solid wastes, we would be composting the wet garbage. Recycling would be easier and would remove more from the waste stream than it currently does. And above all, disposal non-recyclable dry waste does not produce much if any methane gas and leachate byproducts. As a consequence, its disposal would be less environmentally hazardous, less expensive, and less controversial if it were not for all of the other stuff dumped with it.

Yorty's campaign against separating garbage from trash depended on another postwar phenomenon, the dramatic rise in demand for convenience. Convenience costs something. Maybe it costs a lot. Is the benefit is worth the cost? We will never know the answer to that question until we ask it, until we come to understand the costs beyond the purchase price.

It used to be that preparing meals for a family took a woman most of the day, especially back when she had to raise and slaughter whatever animals provided meat and grow her own produce. Nowadays, we can buy, say, lasagna from the freezer section of the grocery store, bread from the deli section, and a bag or two of salad from the produce section. That can provide a complete meal for a family with practically no effort. As a percentage of the family's income, it probably costs less than our great grandparents paid for one of their meals. But consider what we have to pay for besides the food: packaging for the product, packaging for shipping large quantities of product, and wooden pallets to store and move cartons. The raw materials for products and packaging are often located far from the factories. Besides the products and packaging themselves, we pay for transportation of raw materials and packaging to the factory, of products from the factory to the warehouses of various middle men, and of products from the warehouses to stores and/or our homes.

The proliferation of cleaning products

Time was when housewives had to do all of their cleaning with a small number of products, including soap, baking soda, salt, vinegar, ammonia, borax, and lemon juice. At least they could buy soap. Their frontier ancestors had had to make it themselves. As the twentieth century progressed, the trickle of convenience products became a steady stream. My personal memories of it begin with TV commercials in the late 1950s. A Windex™ commercial showed a woman mixing ammonia and water, wrinkling her nose at the awful smell, and sloshing the mixture out of the bucket as she struggled to carry it to the windows. Modern housewives, who switched to Windex, needed only to spray and wipe. The windows got cleaner faster (according to the ads), and the process smelled better, too.

I do not remember the product, but another commercial declared, "Vinegar is for salads." On television, radio, and in print, advertisers made all-out war on the older, more generic products.

New products were supposedly more convenient and more pleasant to use. But each new housekeeping breakthrough only performed one kind of task. Just look at the house-cleaning section of any store today. You'll find

- Detergents that work for laundry
- Detergents that work for dishes, but only if you wash by hand
- Detergents that work for dishes, but only if you use them in a dishwasher
- Products to clean the oven
- Products to clean the floor
- Products to wash windows
- Products to wash counters
- Products to wash walls
- Products to clean the sinks and bathtubs
- Products to clean the toilet
- Products to unclog the drain in sinks and bathtubs
- Products to unclog the toilet
- Products for dusting furniture
- Products for polishing furniture
- Products to make the room smell better
- And more

The commercials worked. Of course, the products did, too, but do they work any better than the old fashioned way? I found it very amusing, several years after I saw the last Windex commercial that tried to persuade housewives to give up ammonia. The new ads began to tout a new formula. Now with ammonia!!! And furniture polishes gushed that they had real lemon juice!!! The familiar smirk that furniture polish has real lemon juice and so many brands of lemonade do not have any started decades ago. I suspect that housewives began to enjoy the new conveniences, but found performance lacking. I know from experience at a store where I once worked that if you mix ammonia and water, apply it liberally to a window, and then use a rubber squeegee to wipe it off, you will not get the streaks that seem to be unavoidable with the spray and wipe cleaners. And what side of the window are the streaks on, anyway? It can take longer to find them than to spray and wipe the window in the first place. Besides being less convenient than advertised, newer products have some steep costs:

- They cost more that the earlier, simpler but more versatile products

- They take more room in kitchen and bathroom cabinets and contribute to clutter. What is the tradeoff if a specialty product saves a little time if the number of them you have makes it hard to find any one of them?
- The greater number of products you take home means a greater amount of packaging you must eventually discard
- Some of them are classified as hazardous wastes when and if you want to discard them
- Even the ones with no hazardous chemicals contribute to water pollution, or at least make the treatment of wastewater more complicated and costly.
- Some of these products contribute to pollution of indoor air. Air fresheners in particular work because of the volatile organic compounds (VOCs) they contain.
- Some VOCs are known allergens and suspected carcinogens. Others are harmless unless mixed with ozone, which has become an unavoidable indoor air pollutant.

Electric dryers, the biggest energy hogs of any household appliance, predate the first Earth Day. Nonetheless, we use them more nowadays. Not long ago, everyone had clotheslines. I remember when I first moved to Chicago in the late 1970s and started taking the el. It went behind lots of three-flat apartment buildings. All of the outside stairways, and the clothes lines attached to them, were exposed to plain view. Actually, I didn't notice the lines themselves unless laundry was hanging on them, but it frequently was.

My mother used the dryer only when it was raining. If she could, she hung the laundry out to dry. Why? Partly because she grew up in the Depression and partly because she liked the smell and feel of line-dried clothes better than what came out of the dryer. We even had clotheslines in the basement so she could at least hang the sheets and pillowcases when it was raining.

Nowadays, she has stopped using clotheslines and uses the dryer all the time. After all, she is in her 90s and needs a cane to walk. But I wonder if that is the only reason there is no longer clothesline in the back yard. There is no neighborhood association there, but plenty of neighborhood associations, especially in the suburbs, forbid clotheslines.

Neighborhoods and house size

When I was in sixth grade or so, I saw the man who lived across the street coming home from wherever he had been. He pulled into our driveway and came in to talk with my parents. Then he got in his car and drove across the street to his own driveway. That seemed very odd. Why not pull into his driveway first and walk across the (dead end) street to our house?

That was at the end of the 1950s. Today, maybe it does not seem odd at all. I did not realize it, but our small-town neighborhood was a new type of neighborhood springing up all over the country at that time. Hardly anything but other people's houses was within walking distance. Such neighborhoods were designed on the assumption that everyone had a car and would drive everywhere. Beginning at that time, many neighborhoods have had no sidewalks, even on busy streets, which discourages even recreational walking. Making walking in the neighborhood inconvenient or even dangerous encourages people to drive even short distances. In other words, instead of moving their bodies they sit. They let the car expend all the energy. Even before every fast food restaurant had a drive-thru lane, our cars were making us fat.

Housing starts between 1945 and 1999 were 350% higher than the earlier part of the century. There were a record 1.9 million housing starts in 1950, of which 1.7 million (88%) were single-family houses. It would take twenty years to surpass that level of activity. On average they had 1065 square feet, 983 square feet of finished space. That figure amounts to about half the size of the 200,000 single family homes built in 1920. Two thirds had only one or two bedrooms, and only 4% had more than one bathroom. Even with half the size of homes built 30 years earlier, there were 8.5 times as many. Building so many homes required land that had previously been open space. The more land used for new houses, the less for agriculture and wildlife habitat.

The small size of new single-family homes in 1950 can be partially explained because the postwar boom had only started and the economy had not fully recovered from the harsher economic conditions of the Depression and the war. Demographics also help to explain the average home size. Men returned from war service and started their families. Men who had not been old enough to serve also started families at the same time. The median age for a first marriage was about 23 for men and 20 for women. These people had never owned homes, and so the vast majority of the homes built that year were starter homes. The homeowner rate in 1950 was 55%.

In 1972, housing starts reached a new record, 2.4 million units, but 44% of that construction was for multi-family housing: apartments or condominiums. The single-family homes built that year had an average finished area of 1634 square feet, a 66% increase from the 1950 average. At least to some extent the newer homes had more rooms: 65% had three or more bedrooms; 23% had four or more bedrooms. Half of them had at least a bathroom and a half. I have not found statistics about lot sizes, but I suspect that these larger houses were built on larger lots. And yet the average household size, the number of people living together in a house, had begun to decrease. Much of the multi-family housing built in the early 1970s was essentially student housing, rented by baby boomers, that is, the very students who provided so much of the energy for the first Earth Day. Multi-family housing was built mostly in already developed areas. The number of new single-family homes was actually less in 1972 than in 1950. Conversion of open space to housing probably remained fairly steady during the interval.

I remember the day I was pushing my noisy gas lawn mower and it dawned on me that modern technology had provided me with a machine so that I could do what used to be the job of the family goat. Zoning regulations would not let me buy a goat even if I especially wanted to. I do not think anyone has ever managed to teach the goat a difference between grass or weeds (eat these) and shrubbery, flowers, or vegetables (don't eat these).

In older urban neighborhoods, houses are very close together. There are lots of tall old trees. Lawns are small, and grass does not grow especially well. It is fairly quick and easy to mow them with a non-motorized reel mower. Over the last sixty years or so, houses are built farther apart on larger tracts of land. We have come to love our big lawns. Those old-fashioned mowers just won't cut it any more (no apology for the pun).

If we cannot shop in our neighborhoods anymore, then we must go someplace else, which means our shopping patterns had to change. I was still in junior high school when Kresge, a failing dime store chain, reinvented itself as Kmart. I do not remember which came first, big box stores or enclosed shopping malls, but both offered the convenience of finding all kinds of products in one place.

And what does it mean to have the big box stores and various kinds of malls gathered in one place in town? Frequent stoplights, confusing traffic patterns, and huge traffic jams. That means not only more gas and time wasted, but also more opportunities for fender-benders. Unlike older neighborhood stores, both big box stores and shopping malls (even little strip malls) require large parking lots. At least those lots make us walk at least a little, but they are impervious to rain. When rain lands on soil, it soaks in, at least until the soil becomes saturated. When it lands on roofs, streets, or parking lots the size of lots of our ancestors' farms, it runs off. It contributes greatly to urban flooding.

Every new convenience is someone's business, someone's livelihood. Of course the company that makes it, whether a large corporation or a small startup, will market it by highlighting its advantages. Consumers ought to weigh the costs and benefits carefully. That would come more naturally if economists and the government did not blame lack of consumer spending for problems in the economy.

Social critics abounded, both in literature and non-fiction. Vance Packard wrote *The Hidden Persuaders, Status Seekers,* and *The Waste Makers.* John Keats wrote *Insolent Chariots* about the auto industry, William Whyte, *Organization Man,* Sloan Wilson novels including *Man in the Gray Flannel Suit* and *Crack in the Picture Window.* Ironically, their works became mass-market best sellers, which the public eagerly consumed and likely discarded after reading them. But they never sold quite as well as titles about home improvement and other subjects to help people become more effective consumers.

Pesticides, pollution, and other environmental problems

Rachel Carson's *Silent Spring* (1962) can be compared with *Uncle Tom's Cabin* as a book that ignited a social movement. Carson did for the environmental movement what Harriet Beecher Stowe had done for abolitionism. Neither woman put forth new ideas, but they introduced the ideas of comparatively small groups of specialists to the general public in a way that not only informed, but inspired by framing the issues as moral issues.

Carson did not start out as an environmentalist. She grew up in Springdale, Pennsylvania, a town with not only a standard coal-fired power plant, but also the American Glue Factory, which slaughtered old horses to make not only glue, but fertilizer. Carson could see its smokestack from her bedroom window. The 1,200 residents of Springdale could not sit on their porches in the evening because of the stench.

I grew up in Bowling Green, Ohio, about two blocks from the Heinz Catsup factory. The stench in the summer could be unbearable. Of course, it mingled with the smell of an open sewage ditch maybe half a mile to the north. Some people liked the Heinz aroma much more than I did. No one liked the ditch. We complained a lot, but at least my generation basically considered it normal. I have seen no indication that Carson thought anything differently about the glue factory. It appears that no one much thought of air pollution or other environmental and public heath issues as national issues until *Silent Spring* came out.

Carson's home life must have caused her greater concern. Her father failed at all of his business ventures. Her older sister worked at the power plant. Her ambitious mother hoped that Rachel could get an education and get out of Springdale. Rachel attended Pennsylvania College for Women (now Chatham University) in Pittsburgh on scholarship. She began graduate study in zoology at Johns Hopkins University and earned a masters degree. She had to drop out before earning a doctorate and return to Springdale to help her family. When the Depression hit, the Carsons fled Springdale, not to get away from the glue factory, but their debt.

Carson eventually joined a New Deal agency, the U.S. Fish and Wildlife Service, as science editor. She also provided freelance articles for The Atlantic and other magazines. Her articles ranged from what to do on summer vacation to the life cycles of sea creatures. Eventually, driven by her love of the ocean, she wrote three best-selling books about it: *The Sea Around Us, The Edge of the Sea,* and *Under the Sea-Wind.*

Meanwhile, Paul Hermann Müller discovered in 1939 that a substance called DDT, first synthesized in 1874, could kill insects. During World War II soldiers applied it to themselves in powder form to control lice. He won the Nobel Prize for this work in 1948. After the war, DDT was sprayed as a fumigant from airplanes onto large land areas, without the owners' permission, to control fire ants and mosquitoes.

Carson became interested in DDT and other synthetic pesticides when wildlife biologists in the U.S. Fish and Wildlife service began to express concerns about its effects on birds and plants. The scientific community began to realize that the chemicals not only killed insects, but animals, birds and fish. DDT weakened birds' eggshells, and some species, such as the osprey, began to die out from inability to reproduce. Housewives had their own concerns, as they witnessed squirrels and birds dying in their backyards after aerial applications of DDT and found their own children getting sick. Dairy farmers in upstate New York whose farms were sprayed to eradicate gypsy moths found their milk banned from the market.

At first, it did not occur to Carson that she should write a book about DDT. She was a naturalist and popular writer about oceans, not an investigative reporter. Writing about the dangers of DDT would pit her against entrenched industrial interests with deep pockets and teams of lawyers, and she was only a single woman. So she tried to interest other authors in writing about the issue. Finally, E. B. White, an editor at *The New Yorker* suggested that she provide some articles for that magazine, which had already serialized her books.

In the early 1960s more Americans were concerned to the point of hysteria about the dangers of radiation and nuclear fallout, a concern much greater than any other environmental issue. Carson drew a direct parallel between the genetic effects of radiation and pesticides. She and Houghton Mifflin, her publisher, knew that such comparisons would spark a firestorm. They attempted to gain some control of the response by sending galleys to the National Audubon Society to get a public endorsement before publication. Its biologist Roland Clement quickly supplied it.

Carson had other important allies. Massachusetts Senator John F. Kennedy, a dedicated yachtsman, knew her two earlier books. Early in his political career he had no particular interest in conservation issues except as they related to the sea. He belonged to the Massachusetts Audubon Society because of his interest in shore birds. He was also a close friend of Supreme Court Justice William O. Douglas, an ardent conservationist who pressed Kennedy to broaden his environmental interests.

During Kennedy's presidential campaign in 1960, Carson served on the Natural Resources Committee of the Democratic Advisory Council, which embraced the environmental advocacy she recommended. She began a campaign to broaden the public's understanding of the environment beyond traditional con-servationism to include public health. While Kennedy read the council's report in October, Jackie Kennedy asked Carson to become a member of the Women's Committee for New Frontiers. Other members included Eleanor Roosevelt and former Secretary of Labor Frances Perkins. Carson spoke persuasively of her research into pesticides to these very influential women.

After its three-part serialization in *The New Yorker* in the summer of 1962, the book appeared on September 27 and immediately became a best seller, selling more than two million copies. It became a Book-of-the-Month Club selection. Eric Severeid interviewed her for CBS Reports. By that time she was so sick from breast cancer that he was not sure she would survive to see the show. She did in fact survive long enough to testify before a Senate subcommittee on pesticides on June 4, 1963. She had to hide her breast cancer from the public to prevent the chemical industry from painting her as a pathetic cancer patient trying to find someone to blame.

Industry responded aggressively. Velsicol, a manufacturer of DDT, threatened legal action against both *The New Yorker* and Houghton Mifflin and attempted to prevent the Audubon Society from publishing excerpts in its magazine. The company's general counsel suggested that Carson was a Soviet employee seeking to reduce Western countries' ability to grow food. Audubon not only published the excerpts, but also an editorial about how the chemical industry had responded, but then declined to endorse *Silent Spring* officially. Velsicol also mounted an aggressive public relations campaign to mock the book and send out information sheets with "facts" that lacked any credible scientific evidence. The chemical industry established the pattern followed since by the tobacco, coal, petroleum, and electric industries among others: spend a lot of money on lawyers, lobbyists, campaign contributions, and public relations; bully opponents by any means available and concede nothing.

By the time Carson finished *Silent Spring* she and the Kennedys were personal friends. Before *The New Yorker* issued its serialization she, the President, and close presidential friends and advisors planned how the administration could help publicize the book and stand up to the inevitable counterattack from industry. As the chemical industry planned its publicity blitz and legal strategy, Kennedy was setting it up as the culprit for so much of what was wrong with the environment. He never directly endorsed *Silent Spring,* but he did announce that because of issues it raised, the Department of Agriculture and the Public Health Service would mount a major investigation to discover if pesticides threatened human health. The chemical industry's attack on *Silent Spring* necessarily became an attack on the President himself. They portrayed him as nothing more than an elitist yachtsman who wanted to take care of his precious national seashore and passively let pesticide manufacturers suffer an unjustified attack. They warned that he risked putting thousands of people out of work.

Kennedy's response to the criticism included awarding a public service gold medal to FDA scientist Frances Oldham Kelsey, who had demonstrated that the popular sedative thalidomide caused birth defects. That action lumped the pharmaceutical industry with the chemical industry as villains whose actions, in Carson's words in an interview put it, "represent our willingness to rush ahead and use something new without knowing what the results are going to be." Kennedy himself had contributed more evidence of that willingness when he authorized using an herbicide nicknamed Agent Orange as a weapon in Vietnam. The Pentagon gave assurance that it would not use defoliants if there appeared to be evidence that they could cause long-term ecological trouble. In fact, Agent Orange was contaminated with dioxins that remained in the soil. After the war they made reforestation difficult or impossible. Invasive weeds took over instead. Agent Orange also caused multiple severe diseases in both the Vietnamese people and American combat veterans.

In her congressional testimony, Carson not only highlighted the problems her book identified, but also presented some policy recommendations, which specifically did not include a ban on DDT, only aerial spraying. She did not advocate federal regulations because of her suspicion that the government's relationship with industry was part of the problem.

She did, however, strongly insist on the public's right to know how pesticides were being used on their property, saying, "If the Bill of Rights contains no guarantee that a citizen shall be secure against lethal poisons distributed either by private individuals or by public officials, it is surely only because our forefathers, despite their considerable wisdom and foresight, could conceive of no such problem" (Griswold 2012). In place of government action, she advocated formation of non-governmental, grassroots citizens groups.

Silent Spring remains controversial. Michael Crichton publically endorsed a comment he put in the mouth of a character in his novel *State of Fear* that "banning DDT killed more people than Hitler." Today the Competitive Enterprise Institute runs the website rachelwaswrong.org, which charges, "Today, millions of people around the world suffer the painful and often deadly effects of malaria because one person sounded a false alarm."

Whether she gets credit or blame for banning DDT, her role has been greatly exaggerated. Manufacture of DDT reached its peak in 1963 and then started to wane, not because of Carson's book, but because of mounting evidence that insects were developing resistance to it. The United States banned DDT for domestic use only in 1972, when Carson had been dead for eight years. American companies continued to export it until the mid-1980s. By 2009, DDT was not manufactured anywhere in the world except India, whose factories produced only 3,653 tons, compared to the 90,000 tons manufactured by American companies alone in 1963.

Simply phasing out one material and replacing it with something else does no good unless the substitute is specifically designed not to cause environmental problems, or at least not the same ones. The substitutes for DDT tended to be other chemicals of the same class, organophosphates. Because they are short-lived, it was necessary to apply them frequently. Insects had already begun to develop immunity to DDT and eventually became immune to the substitutes. Organophosphates are extremely toxic not only to the pests, but the pests' natural enemies and, of course, birds and mammals, including humans. Insecticides in 1970 were ecologically crude largely because chemical companies had scientists who knew how to synthesize them and marketers and salesmen who knew how to sell them, but no one who knew or cared much about their environmental impact.

Carson's scientific claims have held up and remain generally accepted, but she did not originate them. She was a popularizer. She took ideas from the scientific literature and wrote them in a way that resonated with the general public. If people exaggerate Carson's role in eliminating use and manufacture of DDT, it is impossible to exaggerate her effect on public discourse. Earth Day could not have succeeded to the extent it did without her.

Suburbanites discover nature

Aldo Leopold had published *A Sand County Almanac* in 1949, which made many of the same points *Silent Spring* made in 1962, but his book went largely unnoticed. None of the environmental legislation of the 1940s and 50s had required the public to reconsider the impact of American prosperity, consumption, and success on air and water quality and other environmental issues. Three important cultural changes took place in the years separating the two books.

First, as more and more Americans moved to cities and suburbs, fewer of them worked directly with nature, as farmers or miners, for example, to transform natural resources into products. More and more Americans experienced nature only when they left the cities to take part in some kind of recreational activity like hunting, fishing, hiking, or boating. The automobile and airline service had made Americans much more mobile, and they could see much more of the country than individuals of earlier generations. Their very numbers forced one-time environmental skeptics to revise their views that only a few rich hunters cared about conservation issues.

At the same time, Americans wanted to incorporate natural beauty into their home life, with large lawns, the second cultural change. Some social critics began to notice that the growth of suburbs came at the expense of natural open space. Developers named subdivisions after the trees they cut down clear space for them. Folk singer Pete Seeger had a hit record singing "Little Boxes," houses "made out of ticky tacky and they all look just the same." Suburbs full of little boxes far from city centers, where most of the jobs still were, combined the disadvantages of both urban and rural lifestyles without providing any of the advantages of either. Ironically, they bulldozed acre after acre of meadows and woods in order to have a sense of getting back to nature. Parents of baby boomers spent more time and money on child rearing than previous generations and passionately wanted the very best for their offspring. So even as they raped one aspect of nature to make room for their houses, they began to worry about radiation, food safety, and chemicals like no previous generation

Third, even as some people began to count the costs of America's new prosperity on the environment, comfort with that same prosperity prevented them from thinking through their concern to its logical conclusion. They did not trust federal assurances of food safety, for example, but they did not question successive administrations' exhortation to ever increasing consumption. If Americans had maintained traditional thrift and practicality, they would have bought cars, for example, according to their needs for transportation. They would have preferred safe, sturdy, and economical cars, large enough and powerful enough, but not excessively. They never would have thought that changes in exterior design required them to buy new cars frequently in order to stay in style.

DDT was hardly the only chemical that caused public alarm, nor was *Silent Spring* the only cause of apprehension. Indeed, the so-called Delaney Clause in the Food, Drug, and Cosmetic Act of 1958 was a response to the danger of carcinogens in food. The "great cranberry scare," described later, resulted from it.

I mentioned Sam Yorty's campaign against separating garbage earlier in this chapter. What to do about garbage had been a persistent problem for Americans since colonial times. At the end of the 19th century, when people used fireplaces and wood- or coal-burning furnaces, ash accounted for a huge portion of household waste. Horse manure was a major public health issue in towns and cities. Along with other waste from homes, businesses, and factories, it all had to go somewhere, usually a dump. The first incinerators for waste disposal came online shortly before the end of the century. They turned out to be expensive, inefficient, horrendously polluting of both air and water, and foul smelling. Most waste-management incinerators ceased operation before the Great Depression, except in Los Angeles, whose Native-American name means roughly "the land where the campfire smoke never goes away." As most houses in Los Angeles had back yards, most homeowners had their own incinerators until they were outlawed in the late 1950s.

Air and water pollution

Smog arrived in the Los Angeles Basin very early in the 20th century. In 1903, residents thought the thick haze was a solar eclipse. The later vogue for trash incineration, not to mention the city's eventual car culture, only made a bad situation worse. For some reason, no one made a connection between all the burning and the foul air. July 26, 1943 became known as "Black Monday" in Los Angeles. The smog engulfed downtown and reduced visibility to three blocks. The noxious fumes choked pedestrians. A chemical plant bore the brunt of the blame, but air quality did not improve when it was shut down.

Los Angeles may have had the worst overall air quality in the country, but by no means had a monopoly. Killer smog descended on Donora, Pennsylvania for five days, October 26-31, 1948. The town of 14,000 people on the Monongahela River sits in a valley. It is an industrial town, and the sulfuric acid, carbon monoxide, and other pollutants from its steel mills and zinc plant apparently got trapped in a dense fog. Residents who breathed the polluted air began to call local physicians and hospitals. By the time Board of Health head Dr. William Rongaus recommended that people with pre-existing respiratory conditions leave town, 11 elderly people with asthma or heart trouble had already died. Heavy traffic added to the smog and made evacuation difficult. The zinc plant did not shut down until October 31. It started raining later that day, which dispersed the smog. By that time another 9 people had died, raising the death toll to 20, along with thousands of seriously ill people. Air pollution finally became a serious national issue, which led to the passage of the Clean Air Act of 1955.

Decades of raw sewage, industrial waste, agricultural runoff, and household laundry created a vast dead zone in Lake Erie, the shallowest of the Great Lakes. By the 1960s, though, raw sewage was less of a problem. Ironically, treated sewage might have caused even more damage. Sewage technology at the time took advantage of part of the aquatic cycle by converting noxious organic human wastes into inorganic materials. Then it failed to take the other half of the aquatic cycle into account by discharging them into rivers and lakes instead of returning them to the soil. Algae feed on the inorganic material, and when presented with such an abundance of food, proliferated at the expense of the ecosystem as a whole. That explains at least in part how modern technology nearly killed Lake Erie. Large algae blooms in the middle of the lake depleted the oxygen. Nothing could live under their surface. It was declared dead by 1970. Long before that, dead fish washed up on shore all around the lake.

The Cuyahoga River, which empties into the lake in Cleveland, had so much oil and industrial chemicals in it that it actually caught fire on June 22, 1969. Both lake and river became the butt of jokes. As it turns out, however, the iconic photo of the burning river in *Time* was not a picture of the 1969 fire. No one took any, so the magazine had to publish a picture of when the river burned in 1952 with much less publicity.

Households contributed to water pollution every time anyone did a load of laundry. Detergents relied on phosphates, the very substance that killed Lake Erie. Wastewater treatment plants could not deal with phosphates. Fish died in rivers nationwide. Phosphates did not break down in backyard septic tanks or cesspools, either, and eventually seeped into the ground water. Whether from rivers or wells, much of the nation's tap water came with suds. It smelled and tasted bad. Suffolk County, New York, on Long Island banned sale of nearly all detergents, effective March 1, 1971, which only meant that housewives had to drive to a neighboring county to find any. Manufacturers looking for alternatives to phosphates had not yet discovered anything workable.

No one knew for sure if ingesting phosphates in drinking water posed a human health hazard, but a survey by the Department of Health, Education, and Welfare of 939 water systems in 1969 found that many (but by no means most) had dangerous levels of fecal bacteria and heavy metals. It documented cases of illnesses caused by using tap water. Most water systems tested proved adequate, but that was not because of well-trained water system operators or rigorous inspections. More than three quarters of plant operators lacked adequate training. Nearly half did not understand chemistry related to water treatment. Almost 80% of plants were not inspected, and another 10% did not meet whatever government standards existed for frequency of inspection.

Business and government treated the oceans with absolute contempt. Press reports, scholarly articles, official reports of state and federal government commissions all discussed how to extract more resources from the oceans, from seafood to desalted water for human consumption to diamonds. All of this bounty was expected to enrich human life by 2000. At the First International Conference on Waste Disposal in the Sea in 1966 an official involved in developing Los Angeles' sewer outfalls spoke of the "great economy inherent in the discharge of urban sewage and industrial wastes into near-shore waters for final disposal" (Hedgpeth, 1970). After all, "Its vast area and volume, its oxygen-laden waters, its lack of potability or usefulness for domestic and most industrial purposes, present an unlimited and most attractive reservoir for waste assimilation."

Joel W. Hedgpeth. Resident Director of the Marine Science Center at Oregon State University, recalled writing gloomy assessments of environmental matters, to the annoyance of his old English professor. He claimed a sense of personal vindication when the English professor himself published a book about the problems of getting rid of garbage. He compared the attitude of sanitary engineers eager to use the ocean for dumping with the general lack of concern over how to dispose of nuclear wastes.

Here is a single example of nuclear waste, as it relates to oceans: Starting in 1952, low-level radioactive wastes were released into the Columbia River at Hanford, 250 miles upstream from the ocean, and carefully monitored to ensure that the discharge did not exceed permissible levels of radioactivity established for edible seaweed. No such levels had been established for permissible levels that people who ate seafood might accumulate in their bodies.

Hedgpeth also drew an analogy with automobile exhaust. It had been recognized as extremely poisonous since a study published in 1923, which urged taking legal measures to regulate it. An automobile industry official had remarked that his company was in the business of making and selling cars, and that it would not conform to any requirement to deal with health hazards unless compelled by law. It became impossible 46 years later to avoid news stories about polluted air and editorial demands that something be done. Yet in 1968, based on nothing that constituted scientific research or engineering studies, someone seriously proposed tunneling under mountains and the San Andreas Fault so that central California would have access to the ocean for waste disposal!

By far the largest and most spectacular instance of water pollution that led up to the first Earth Day occurred off the coast of Santa Barbara, California. A Union Oil platform six miles offshore blew out on January 28, 1969. Capping the initial leak took 11 days, but the oil slick continued to grow. Upon further investigation, oil was pouring from multiple ruptures on the ocean floor that cumulatively poured 4,000 gallons of oil into the ocean every day for several months. Workers reduced the flow to 315 gallons a day by June, but oil continued to leak at that rate for the rest of the year. Most of the oil was concentrated in the 35-mile stretch of coast nearest the ruptures, but patches of oil drifted as far south as the Mexican border and as far north as Pismo Beach. Thousands of oil-soaked birds also washed ashore.

The federal government responded slowly. On February 26 Secretary of Interior Walter Hickel called for stiffer environmental laws to protect offshore areas. President Nixon visited Santa Barbara and promised to send federal troops if necessary, but not until March 21, after the bulk of the major cleanup had concluded. The cleanup effort did not include any kind of boom to prevent oil from reaching the beaches. Bulldozers collected what washed ashore. Cleanup crews did use some detergent to break it up, which might have done as much harm as good. The process also entailed steam cleaning rocks—and thereby cooking the mussels attached to them.

A newer issue had begun to heat up at about the same time, the race to build the supersonic transport (SST). Conservation organizations including Friends of the Earth, the Sierra Club, the Wilderness Society joined with the Citizens League Against the Sonic Boom formed a coalition to block American participation in its development. Why subject the entire nation to sonic booms in order to save a few hours travel time for a very small fraction of the flying public?

Environmental law, 1945-1970

The conservation movement can be traced back at least as far as the creation of Yellowstone National Park during the Grant administration. It reached its high water mark in influence during the presidency of Theodore Roosevelt. Four national conservationist groups existed by the end of the Second World War.

The oldest, the Sierra Club was founded in 1892 by John Muir over the issue of defeating a proposal to reduce the size of Yosemite National Park to make room for business use of the land. Its first big issue, therefore, was preserving wilderness areas and making them accessible for people to enjoy. It unsuccessfully opposed building of the Hetch Hetchy Dam within Yosemite, wanted by San Francisco as a water supply, in 1907. After Muir's death, the Sierra Club successfully advocated the establishment of the National Park Service to protect the growing number of national parks and monuments. It still had to fight to defeat subsequent attempts to build dams within national parks. It did not have a chapter outside California until organization of the Atlantic Chapter in 1950. Today the Sierra Club has expanded its concerns far beyond wilderness preservation, but that evolution only started in 1969

The Massachusetts Audubon Society formed in 1896 over outrage at the slaughter of egrets and other waterfowl to provide feathers for ladies' hats. The National Audubon Society formed as a coalition of existing state groups in 1901. It has focused its conservations efforts primarily on birds, but has moved from protesting hats to advocating for the conservation and restoration of natural ecosystems.

The Izaak Walton League was founded in 1922 by a gathering of 54 sportsmen concerned about deterioration of the nation's top fishing streams because of discharges of raw sewage and industrial wastes and soil erosion. It also raised issues of draining wetlands, the destruction of forests and wilderness areas and otherwise causing the disappearance of wildlife habitats. Named for the 17th-century author of *The Compleat Angler,* it is an organization of anglers, hunters, and other outdoorsmen dedicated to taking action to resolve these problems. Some of its members served in Congress and participated in creating the landmark environmental legislation of the 1940s.

Jay Norwood "Ding" Darling – cartoonist by profession and conservationist as a hobby, noted that "wildlife doesn't vote, neither do conservationists." Appointed Chief of the Bureau of Biological Survey (which later became the Fish and Wildlife Service), he resigned after several frustrating years of political battles. At that time he persuaded President Franklin Roosevelt to convene the first North American Wildlife Conference in Washington, DC in 1936. The National Wildlife Federation, the newest of the four major conservation groups was born from that meeting. The 2,000 participants organized state federations. It unites hunters and anglers with bird watchers, scientists, outdoor enthusiasts, and families in a single organization.

Membership of traditional conservation groups was mostly white and relatively wealthy. The Los Angeles chapter of the Sierra Club had rejected black membership as recently as 1959. The groups had to be careful to preserve their tax-exempt status in order to get sufficient donations. Since they had traditionally concentrated on preserving the wilderness, when the need to tackle urban problems became evident, they did not know how to do it.

The Franklin Roosevelt administration's tactics for battling the Depression included rural electrification and building dams to supply hydropower, beginning with the establishment of the Tennessee Valley Authority. The U.S. Army Corps of Engineers took leadership in developing and building dams. It claimed to take every action necessary to protect the rivers. Every state had its own conservation department, which rejected that assertion, but had little power to do anything about it. The Truman administration continued the policy and envisioned building dams throughout the watersheds of the Missouri, Columbia, and Mississippi Rivers.

The first major postwar environmental clash took place between conservationists and dam builders. Before the end of the war, conservationists had simply begged dam builders to care about nature. Now it was time to demand. Kenneth Reid, executive director of the Izaak Walton League, complained, "The Army Engineers Corps and the Bureau of Reclamation are both scouring the country like a swarm of locusts trying to find every possible site for a dam" (Brooks 2009). He warned that these two agencies would destroy salmon runs in the Pacific. Since most league members lived in the Midwest or Northeast, his advocacy of Northwestern fisheries underscored the growing national vision of conservationists.

A lone conservationist in Congress

In contrast, hardly anyone at the federal level cared much about the issue of conservation. The primary exception was Virginia Representative and later Senator A. Willis Robertson. He was already an ardent naturalist when he began his legislative career as a Virginia state senator in the 1920s and served as the first chairman of the state's Game and Inland Fisheries Commission. He used those positions to battle Virginia's paper industry, which wanted to put a dam on the James River. Robertson argued that the publicized reason for the dam, reliable drinking water, simply covered the industry's use of the river as an open sewer to dilute the toxic wastewater it poured into it.

Robertson entered the U.S. House of Representatives in 1932 as loyal New Dealer, and quickly secured a political base of operations for promoting conservation by persuading the House to create the Select Committee on Wildlife Conservation and naming him chair. From there he continued to oppose dam projects and criticize the Army Corps of Engineers. In 1937, along with Sen. Key Pittman of Nevada, he sponsored the Wildlife Restoration Act, also known as the Pittman-Robinson Act, which imposed an excise tax on guns and sporting ammunition to provide federal funding for state conservation agencies. He was elected senator in 1946 and served three terms. He could always find allies in both houses and both parties, but he seems to have been alone in taking initiative on environmental issues.

When the war in the Pacific ended in 1945, Robertson urged conservationists to lead a national debate on the place of nature in the nation's priorities. Scientists, wildlife managers, and sportsmen in their various ways called attention to the ecological damage that resulted from Depression-era funding cuts for research and publication, New Deal public works, wartime mobilization, and lax enforcement of existing law. Robertson enlisted support of the Izaak Walton League. He encouraged members to broaden their appeal to other aspects of outdoor recreation and link conservation to public health and, as a firm states rights politician, the preservation of democracy.

A report by The Wildlife Federation, which could only have been written with Robertson's help, warned that few national leaders with high positions in the military or civil government cared about conservation. Robertson urged conservation professionals in state government and private citizens who cared about conservation to put pressure on federal officials. Water quality and pollution became their rallying cry.

In 1946 Robertson proposed the Fish and Wildlife Conservation Act (FWCA) to require dam-builders to submit their plans to scientists and citizens. Before it could become law he had to overcome fierce opposition from the Army Corps of Engineers and persuade President Truman to sign it. To that end, he organized and coordinated pressure on the President from national conservation groups and state conservation officials. Truman's cabinet gave him conflicting advice. Federal Power Commission chair Leland Olds warned that FWCA "would have an unduly hampering effect on full conservation, control, and use of the nation's water resources" and urged him to veto it. But Secretary of Interior Julius Krug reminded Truman that an extremely large cross-section of the public shared an interest in wildlife and that FWCA's mandatory review process would enable the federal government to work more closely with state governments. Krug's support of the act persuaded War

Secretary Robert Patterson to reconsider his opposition to the act. It also reminded Truman that 18 million sportsmen represented voters he needed on his side in the 1946 midterm elections. Passage of the act marked a major turning point in environmental law.

Robertson also led passage of two other important environmental laws: the Federal Insecticide, Fungicide, and Rodenticide Act (FIFRA, 1947) and the Federal Water Pollution Control Act (FWPCA, 1948). He won key battles with dam builders, but by the mid-1960s felt powerless against suburban expansion, which made fortunes for developers, builders, and bankers. He never sympathized with the new brand of environmentalism inspired by *Silent Spring*.

One unintended consequence of FWCA: environmental activists had won a mandate for government agencies to perform studies, but rather than simply accepting the results of the studies, activists critiqued them and pitted scientific expertise against the expertise of government agencies. The controversies triggered a new round of statutes and the process of review and criticism continued. Environmental lawmaking, both legislatively and administratively, required gathering of data, funding new research, and solicitation of public comment in hope of reaching a fact-based consensus. The process has rarely if ever resulted in resolution of any problem, old or new. But before FWCA, environmentalists had no mechanism for questioning administrative positions or causing administrators to come to grips with the environmental consequences of their decisions.

Although state governments continued to write more water quality law than the federal government, the FWPCA had established federal primacy in establishing interstate standards under authority of the Interstate Commerce Clause of Article I and the Supremacy Clause of Article VI of the U.S. Constitution. States enacted their laws under federal directives. The various water quality acts became legal precedent for similar federalization of air pollution control. Increasing federal power eroded the Tenth Amendment, which defines states rights. (Opponents of civil rights and civil rights laws regularly invoked the Tenth Amendment to the extent that progressives have managed to persuade the public that states rights is nothing but a code word for racist intentions.)

In the wake of the killer fog in Donora, Pennsylvania President Truman ordered the Public Health Service to investigate and report on the tragedy. It recommended nothing more substantial than study and research. Otherwise, Truman responded to the air pollution issue with inability to dodge public pressure but passive unwillingness to seek legislation to deal with it. The public was unwilling to wait for federal legislation, and once again activists had more success getting laws passed by states and large cities. They rejected industry claims that anti-pollution legislation violated businesses' property rights.

By 1951, large cities from coast to coast (Los Angeles, St. Louis, Cleveland, Pittsburgh, and New York) had enacted tough local air quality ordinances. The states of New Jersey and Maryland had authorized studies in preparation for state air quality laws. California had passed its Air Pollution Control Act in 1947. Congress did not pass any federal air quality legislation until 1963.

State environmental statutes frequently made it to the Supreme Court, where two opposing viewpoints skirmished over how to reconcile two postwar legislative innovations with the Constitution. On the one hand, FWCA and subsequent environmental laws had given federal administrative agencies new lawmaking power. On the other hand, the Administrative Procedure Act had required the courts to guarantee citizens' constitutional rights, including property rights. Industry claimed that state environmental laws violated their property rights. Two Supreme Court justices, Felix Frankfurter and William O. Douglas, who was becoming an ardent conservationist, were waging a battle, both personal and philosophical, over how much weight public opinion should have in judicial decisions. Frankfurter, who favored law-making administrators over law-making judges, usually produced a majority that consistently struck down state environmental laws.

Renewed concern for food safety

Federal laws sometimes conflicted with each other. Food safety had been a public issue since before the publication of *The Jungle* by Upton Sinclair in 1906. The federal Food and Drug Act became law in 1905. The Insecticide Act followed in 1910, the nation's first pesticide law, to protect both the food supply and farmers. FIFRA, its replacement, was intended to establish national standards. It required manufacturers of chemicals to register them with the U.S. Department of Agriculture, sell them with proper warning labels, and renew the registration every five years. By 1970, it had not so much limited the manufacture and sale of toxic and hazardous chemicals as protected it. Although the law provided procedures for refusing to register a chemical and revoking registrations once offered, the Department's Pesticides Registration Division never once did so.

The administrative gutting of FIFRA's intent caused a clash with the Food and Drug Administration. A 1938 amendment to the Food and Drug Act had given it power to establish limitations on the amount of pesticides food could contain before it became "adulterated" and unfit for sale. As agriculture became a chemical-dependent industry, the food industry had a growing concern about the clash between FIFRA and the older Food and Drug Act. The Eisenhower administration attempted to broker a deal among chemical manufacturers, farmers, food processors, and grocers that became the Miller Amendment to the Food and Drug Act (1954). Among other things, it empowered the FDA to establish zero tolerance for certain chemicals and forbid the sale of any food that had any detectable quantity of it. The Delaney Clause to regulate food additives followed in 1958, forbidding the use in food of any substance known to cause cancer in either humans or lab animals. Careless interpretation of that clause led to the great cranberry scare of 1959. It shows tension between different agencies of government, as the USDA had licensed the herbicide in 1958 according to FIFRA because it dissipated quickly and did not harm the wetlands cranberries grow in.

In November of that year an FDA ruling led Secretary of Health, Education, and Welfare Arthur S. Fleming to invoke the clause for the first time. He warned consumers that traces of aminotriazole, a weed killer and not an additive, had been found in cranberries grown in Oregon and Washington. He urged Americans to avoid eating cranberries until the new crop could be tested, just to be safe. That crop had set records for abundance, and cranberry growers anticipated record sales. It was, of course, impossible to complete the tests between then and Thanksgiving. Fleming's warning resulted in record low sale of cranberries.

Fleming based his warning on three serious errors in judgment. First, the herbicide was found only in those two states, which produced only a small portion of the nation's cranberry crop. Second, later research determined that only a miniscule amount had been found. Third, Fleming completely misread the clause, which prohibited the sale of *food* that contained dangerous chemicals. Aminotriazole had been detected in raw cranberries, not in any finished cranberry products available for sale.

Urging Americans to "be on the safe side," or to use a more recent term, use "an abundance of caution," often serves as a call to cowardice in the face of a very minor threat. Grocery stores removed cranberry products from their shelves. Restaurants removed them from menus. Some towns even passed ordinances to ban the sale of cranberry products. The Eisenhower administration responded to the panic with a compromise that essentially papered over the tension. Mrs. Fleming eventually had to invite television crews to her house to film the family eating unsprayed cranberries to prove they were safe to eat.

Congress soon gave the industry almost $10 million to compensate growers for their losses. The cranberry scare lasted only that one season, and sales returned to normal the following year. The public's irrational fear of the food supply did not go away as quickly. To be sure, there have been plenty of legitimate food recalls in the face of life-threatening contamination, but the legacy of the cranberry scare remains, as seen in subsequent health panics that have turned out to have no basis in fact.

No important environmental legislation was enacted during the Kennedy administration, but he and Lyndon Johnson after him shared more enthusiasm for environmental issues than any President since Theodore Roosevelt. That Kennedy was willing to risk political capital to defend Rachel Carson and take on the wrath of the chemical industry shows a new regulatory attitude that may have been more important than legislation. President Kennedy's Science Advisory Committee issued its report on May 15, 1963 and recommended that the government undertake a public education campaign to warn about the dangers of pesticides. Carson and others in the private sector had long been able to generate public interest in environmental issues. As President Johnson continued to support Kennedy's environmental initiatives, the administration itself began to appeal directly to the public.

Environmental law activity before Earth Day produced some landmark federal legislation, which demonstrates both the interest in environmental matters and the variety of issues Congress and the public worked on:

- Fish and Wildlife Coordination Act, (1946)
- Federal Insecticide, Fungicide, and Rodenticide Act (1947)
- Federal Water Pollution Control Act (1948)
- Food and Drug Act "Miller Amendment" (1954) and "Delaney Clause" (1958)

- Air Pollution Control Act (1955)
- Fish & Wildlife Act (1956)
- Water Pollution Control Act (1956)
- Hazardous Substances Control Act (1960)
- Clean Air Act (1963)
- Motor Vehicle Pollution Control Act (1965)
- Shoreline Erosion Protection Act (1965)
- Solid Waste Disposal Act (1965)
- Endangered Species Act (1966)
- Federal Air Quality Act (1967) – the 1970 Clean Air Act was not new legislation, but an amendment to this and 1963 acts.
- National Environmental Policy Act (signed by President Nixon on nationwide television January 1, 1970)

Conservationists become environmentalists

Meanwhile, conservationists, beginning to prefer the term "environmentalist" because of recently expanded goals, became more and more militant, believing that America would destroy itself if it didn't change attitudes towards the environment. More and more Americans were beginning to agree. The Sierra Club and National Audubon Society had both doubled their membership in just three or four years. Friends of the Earth, a new group, organized as a lobbying group, with no tax exemption for contributions.

The Citizen's Crusade for Clean Water encouraged Congress to vote for $800 million for pollution control instead of the $214 million the Nixon administration requested. Besides the various conservation groups, the coalition included the U.S. Conference of Mayors, the League of Women Voters, AFL-CIO, United Auto Workers, and the National Rifle Association. Alliances like that gave the environmental movement political muscle it had never had before. The John Birch Society and Students for a Democratic Society agreed completely on the desirability of clean air and water. Students were recent parts of the coalition, having been rarely seen at conservation meetings even a year earlier.

The Sierra Club expanded its priorities beyond wilderness protection to include pollution, pesticides, urban planning, and population control in Fall 1969. It had initiated 55 legal actions nationwide and obtained injunctions against five of Nixon's cabinet members. The National Audubon Society expanded its mission from saving endangered birds to saving the endangered human race and assembled a coalition that stopped construction of a jetport in the Everglades.

Environmentalists feared that all efforts to improve the environment would be in vain unless America abandoned its drive to be a nation of plenty based on growing consumption. They not only wanted to stop misusing natural resources, but also restrain technological progress. Population control had become the ultimate environmentalist goal. Environmentalists increased militancy resulted in stormy confrontations with bureaucrats and business leaders. Their chosen battleground was the court system. They found judges more receptive to change—implicitly more receptive than elected officials. They needed to bring about a new legal framework not limited to suing for private damages. Common law concepts were not responsive to the new tactic of suing on behalf of the public interest, so conservationists needed new precedents in court.

The Scenic Hudson Preservation Conference sued the New York utility Consolidated Edison in 1964 to halt construction of a 2 million-kilowatt pumped storage plant that would have damaged historic and scenic areas along the river. They won the case the following year in the Second Circuit of the U.S. Court of Appeals, and the Supreme Court declined to hear the utility's appeal. The decision gave conservationists two important precedents. First, it overruled the Federal Power Commission's contention that they lacked legal standing to intervene in hearings because they could not demonstrate personal economic interests at stake. Second, it ruled that the Commission had an affirmative duty to gather information on its own in order to protect the public interest. The Commission had neglected to study the environmental effects of the proposed plant or any available alternatives.

At about the same time, a local environmental group, the village of Tarrytown, New York, and the Sierra Club sued the Army Corps of Engineers, the U.S. Secretary of Transportation, and the New York Commissioner of Transportation in a district court to get an injunction against Governor Nelson Rockefeller's plan to build a six-lane highway along the river. The court ruled that the kind of structures the Army Corps of Engineers proposed to build violated the Rivers and Harbors Act of 1899. It held that the Corps was wrong not to seek congressional permission and found that even though no statutory provision for court review existed, the Corps did not have "sovereign immunity" to protect it from litigation.

The Environmental Defense Fund, started in 1966 to stop spraying of DDT in public places, had a mission to make public policy take science into account. It accepted only cases the scope of the two Hudson River cases, but acted nationwide. It combined scientific caution and daring legal innovation. It also sought to counteract the weight of government and industrial expert witnesses by creating a pool of 300 scientists to serve as volunteer expert witnesses.

Waging environmental war in the courts achieved an act of Congress forbidding any federally licensed or financed projects along the Hudson River unless the Department of Interior determined that a project would do no harm to the river's resources. But it had two important limitations. First, it was expensive. Second, the courts could change government procedures, but it could not give legal definitions to environmental problems. The criminal code can outlaw any kind of stealing, for example, but an environmental code could never outlaw all dam or highway building,

Because the state of the environment had captured the public imagination, it was the safest possible political issue. No one admitted to being opposed to conservation. In 1969, the Nixon administration trailed the rest of the country in concern for the environment because it concentrated so much attention on Vietnam. But as the 1970s began, he was beginning to take environmental leadership and put the issue on the top of his agenda.

Chapter 2 Earth Day: Planning, Execution, Immediate Results

Earth Day—idea and planning

Earth Day was the brainchild of Wisconsin Senator Gaylord Nelson. Nelson had tried to ignite interest in environmental issues first as Governor of Wisconsin in the early 1960s and later as senator. He introduced legislation to the Senate to protect wild rivers, clean up the Great Lakes, and to ban chemicals like DDT and non-biodegradable detergents. His colleagues were not interested.

But just as Rachel Carson get too much of both credit and blame for the abandonment of DDT, it appears that Nelson himself took too much personal credit for Earth Day. I have found an article he wrote looking back on it, but it was posted on the web without a date. He wrote that the idea had been in his mind since 1962, although he gave no credit to the publication of *Silent Spring* that year. He had already been troubled, he wrote, for several years that environmental issues were not an important political issue. In November 1962 he approached the President with the idea of a national conservation tour, as if Kennedy were not already actively collaborating with Carson. The President spoke on environmental issues in eleven states in September 1963, but according to Nelson, nothing much came of it at the time. Senator Nelson continued to speak out on his own. People cared. Other politicians didn't.

Nelson did not acknowledge the pioneering work of his colleague from Virginia, Willis Robertson, although by that time Robertson had made himself known more as a segregationist than conservationist. He did not acknowledge the important environ-mental legislation passed in the 13 years before 1960s

But if he took undue credit for being the lone political advocate for the environment, he did conceive the idea that made it an unavoidable issue. In 1969, Nelson witnessed the effects of the Santa Barbara oil spill. At the same time, grassroots opposition to the war in Vietnam was growing. Nelson saw an opportunity to channel the same kind of energy to force politicians to consider environmental issues. The idea for Earth Day was born.

When he started paying attention to antiwar teach-ins in August 1969, he recognized that they provided a model to empower people to take action, and not incidentally, to spur the government to action. Whether he knew it or not, students from most of the largest universities in the country had already met in July 1969 at the University of Wisconsin to plan similar activities related to the environment. Nelson announced a national teach-in on the environment to the Annual Symposium of the Washington Environmental Council in Seattle in September 1969. He expressed fear that it was already too late to persuade the "establishment" of the seriousness of the environmental crisis.

Nelson, a Democrat, invited Republican Congressman Paul McCloskey to assist him as co-chairman of the national committee, which included the president of The Conservation Foundation, Stanford University biology professor Paul Ehrlich, one other academic, and three students. The committee took out a full-page advertisement in the *New York Times* to begin its campaign both to stimulate interest and raise money. The Sierra Club had announced the teach-in in its national news report of December 12, 1969. *Newsweek* devoted the entire education column of its December 22, 1969 issue to students' planning. The *New York Times* had already started coverage by the end of November. Press coverage remained strong through the completion of Earth Day events.

A Democratic Party operative had advised Nelson to organize the teach-in from the top down and maintain personal control over its planning and execution. Instead he decided to build it as a grassroots movement and give as many people as possible a sense of ownership. That decision, more than any other single decision he made, fostered Earth Day's phenomenal success. It was only in November, after having put in 16-hour workdays for months, that he decided to set up a separate entity, Environmental Teach-In Inc. It opened in December with seed money from the Conservation Foundation, the United Auto Workers, and other entities, under the direction of Denis Hayes, a Harvard Law student. Nelson did not coin the term "Earth Day." The students in his Environmental Teach-In Inc. did. This group renamed itself Environmental Action after Earth Day and formed as a non-tax exempt lobbying group.

Hayes had been an active and confrontational student body of Stanford University. He considered environmentalism and antiwar activism as facets of the same struggle for social change. He assembled a team of like-minded veteran civil rights and antiwar activists, the oldest of whom was 28. One organized schools. Four others served as regional coordinators. As Hayes conceived his organization, the staff would provide ideas and contact for local organizers, but he quickly discovered that organization of local events was well underway in many places before the national group was open for business. Instead of taking direction and getting suggestions from the national office, local organizers informed the national staff of their progress. The national office therefore became a clearinghouse for information, a central location where the news media could learn of plans anywhere in the country.

Some people apparently welcomed a discussion of environmental issues, hoping it would be a quieting force to heal wounds on troubled campuses. Hayes called their attention to a conflict of values between those who care about a better world and those who care only for bigger, faster, and more profitable. He warned that greater division would result if corporations or politicians who piously advocated environmental change refused to take action to enact necessary programs. Other people feared the prospect of the environmental movement distracting people from other concerns like racial oppression or war. Hayes would have none of it. All of those issues were facets of the same problem (Hayes 1970).

Hayes dismissed the pre-existing conservationist groups. He charged they had been fighting losing battles for half a century because corporate decision makers responded to their protests of environmental destruction only through their public relations departments. In the few months since the April teach-ins were announced, he pointed out that companies had placed a record number of full-page ads before the public touting their battle for a quality environment, but had not really done anything.

Hayes frequently quoted Robert Kennedy, whose 1968 speech on the gross national product anticipated the concerns Earth Day dealt with.

> The gross national product includes air pollution and advertising for cigarettes, and ambulances to clear our highways of carnage. It counts special locks for our doors, and jails for the people who break them. The gross national product includes the destruction of the redwoods and the death of Lake Superior. It grows with the production of napalm and missiles and nuclear warheads.
>
> And if the gross national product includes all this, there is much that it does not comprehend. It does not allow for the health of our families, the

quality of their education or the joy of their play. It is indifferent to the decency of our factories and the safety of our streets alike. It does not include the beauty of our poetry or the strength of our marriages, the intelligence of our public debate or the integrity of our public officials... The gross national product measures neither our wit nor our courage, neither our wisdom nor our learning, neither our compassion nor our devotion to country. It measures everything, in short, except that which makes life worthwhile, and it can tell us everything about America - except whether we are proud to be Americans (Hayes 1970).

In testimony before the House Subcommittee on Conservation and Natural Resources Hayes said

Most of the politicians and businessmen who are jumping on the environmental bandwagon haven't the slightest idea what they're getting into. They don't realize that we are going to need values.... This country consumes resources at an extravagant rate and gags on its own garbage. Something is drastically wrong. Pollution is only one symptom of the environmental crisis in this nation. We are spending insanely large sums on military hardware instead of eliminating hunger and poverty. We squander resources on moon dust while people live in wretched housing, and we still waste money and lives in a war we should never have entered. (Carter March 20, 1970)

The local coordinators were a diverse group. Some were the same housewives that Rachel Carson realized were her natural allies. Their concern for the environment grew out of their experience as mothers and homemakers. Other coordinators included politicians or young doctors, lawyers and other young professionals. At least in Cleveland, planning for Earth Day came from the mayor's office. At universities, coordinators were usually but not always students, including graduate students in the sciences and undergraduate leaders of student government. Teachers and children shared responsibility for organizing events at their schools.

An overview of Earth Day

Earth Day succeeded beyond anyone's expectations. Before moving on to details of activities, it helps to look at its overall magnitude. To begin with, not all of them occurred on April 22. Events began in January. In many locations they spread out over an entire week.

In an era of mass protest movements and other large gatherings, Earth Day dwarfed them all. Twice as many people participated in New York City alone than attended Woodstock. No demonstration against the Vietnam War, no civil rights demonstration, no feminist demonstration came close to either the numbers or variety of participants, even if their coordinators for these other issues arranged for simultaneous protests in multiple cities. Hayes estimated that Earth Day was easily five times larger than any antiwar rally and twenty times larger than any civil rights demonstration (Hayes 2005).

Few people could have been considered environmental experts in 1970, but people from all walks of life had concerns and eagerly seized the chance to express them. The number of people who spoke at Earth Day events probably exceeded 35,000. Millions off people listened to all the speeches and volunteered time to organized and coordinate events.

Academics representing a wide variety of disciplines comprised the largest group of speakers. Bureaucrats from federal, state, and local governments probably came in a respectable second. The U.S. Department of Interior alone sent a thousand people to speak at the various events. Congress took the day off so its members could speak, and more than 60% took advantage. Several governors gave Earth Day addresses, as did thousands of state legislators, mayors, city counselors, county commissioners, and so on. Participants included Republicans and Democrats, business leaders and union leaders, educated and uneducated, urban people, suburban people, and rural people. Business leaders (mostly local), union leaders, religious leaders, celebrities, community organizers, housewives, and school children all eagerly took their turns addressing crowds. Earth Day pulled Americans together like nothing else short of a catastrophe. Yet it was revolutionary.

Issues of civil rights, women's rights, and Vietnam had energized college campuses for a few years before Earth Day, and organizers were careful to tie environmental issues to the others. Young people, the baby boom generation, took major responsibility for planning Earth Day activities and made a large portion of the people who attended them. In a way, environmental issues belonged to that generation more than to their parents and grandparents. They were the first generation to have unnatural substances like DDT and radioactive strontium 90 in their bones and fat. Many authors who wrote about Earth Day activities and the planning that led to them expressed the hope that these young people would carry on environmental activism for the rest of their lives and make a permanent difference in society.

Environmental issues were new to public discourse. None of the speakers had a body of clichés and platitudes to fall back on. Everyone opposed pollution, but no one yet had a vision of what an environmental movement should look like or what it should try to accomplish. Speakers proposed multiple descriptions of environmental problems, their causes and solutions. Earth Day united two movements that had been separate before. The conservation movement grew largely from hunters and fishers, who realized that their prey's habitat had to thrive if the animal and fish population could thrive. Urban dwellers for whom the wilderness meant scenery likewise supported it. Conservationists could not boast large numbers of people, but they had achieved considerable success in preserving natural areas.

The other movement had no name and no recognition as a movement, but looking back we can recognize the beginnings of the environmental health movement in the 1950s, when distinguished scientists like Linus Pauling and philosophers like Bertrand Russell began to speak out. They called attention to the dangers of radiation from atmospheric tests of nuclear weapons. This movement gathered steam with Rachel Carson's warnings about pesticides. Earth Day also attracted people concerned about such other issues as lead poisoning, the SST, overconsumption, and especially overpopulation.

In addition, Earth Day brought the relatively unknown science of ecology to public consciousness. Many people spoke and wrote of "the ecology" as if it were a synonym of "the environment," even some environmental scientists who should have known better. In fact, ecology is the study of the interactions of plants and animals in ecosystems. Undoubtedly many people who took part in Earth Day activities soon lost interest and moved on to other issues as soon as the excitement of events subsided. For others involvement in Earth Day was life changing, causing them to reconsider career and lifestyle choices. I suppose that for a majority of people, Earth Day sparked a much less intense interest but nevertheless one that continued to shape their opinions and choices years into the future.

Barry Commoner, professor of plant physiology at Washington University and a prominent voice on environmental matters might be representative of how many different scientists first became advocates for the environment. He wrote that he did not start out as ecologist, but as a cellular biologist. The close link he observed between the problems of war and environment pushed him to change his emphasis to ecology. In the 1950s, the Atomic Energy Commission gave the nation repeated assurance that the radioactive fallout from nuclear tests was harmless. Commoner and other scientists began to test the assertion and discovered that radiation was indeed harmful both to humans and whatever ecosystem it encountered. That issue also taught him that, because science is part of society, scientists have a debt to society to look after the social consequences of scientific research (Commoner April 4, 1970).

The Vietnam War demonstrated to Commoner another link between war and environmental issues. President Eisenhower had warned of the military-industrial complex, and even after the end of the Second World War, industry depended heavily on the diversion of human and natural resources from meeting human needs to the military.

He warned the environmental outlook was grim and perilous, and insisted that the overriding question facing the world was how humanity could survive. The challenge also presented an opportunity to learn to use science to live with nature, not dominate it, to discover how to use science and technology so that the world could reap their benefits and avoid threats of the consequences of their misuse.

Because Senator Nelson announced Earth Day six months in advance, the media had plenty of time to prepare. Many high-circulation magazines wrote cover stories about environmental issues by the end of February, even *Sports Illustrated*. Only a few newspapers regularly covered environmental issues before 1970. Over the course of that year, many others began to assign reporters to them. In addition, newspapers also covered Earth Day preparations and published special sections on the environment in April. The coming occasion was largely absent from television until April, but then all of the networks gave special coverage to it. Both networks and local stations offered special programming on Earth Day itself. Book publishers also issued dozens of titles, many of them mass market paperbacks, devoted to some aspect or other of the environment, the environmental movement, and the new environmental activism.

Later, Nelson wrote,

It was obvious that we were headed for a spectacular success on Earth Day. It was also obvious that grassroots activities had ballooned beyond the capacity of my U.S. Senate office staff to keep up with the telephone calls, paper work, inquiries, etc. In mid-January, three months before Earth Day, John Gardner, Founder of Common Cause, provided temporary space for a Washington, D.C. headquarters. I staffed the office with college students and selected Denis Hayes as coordinator of activities.

Earth Day worked because of the spontaneous response at the grassroots level. We had neither the time nor resources to organize 20 million demonstrators and the thousands of schools and local communities that participated. That was the remarkable thing about Earth Day. It organized itself (Nelson undated).

Teach-Ins and other activities

The first environmental teach-in of 1970 took place at Northwestern University beginning on Friday evening, January 23 and ran over night. Speakers included future Senator Adlai Stevenson III (a Democrat), Illinois Attorney General William Scott (a Republican), Barry Commoner, and Paul Ehrlich.

Earth Day activities first achieved national news coverage with the teach-in at the University of Michigan March 11-15. More than 50 teach-in organizers visited Ann Arbor from other campuses, including Hayes. The University of Michigan was the site of the first Vietnam Teach-In. It is therefore entirely appropriate that its Environmental Teach-in predated the official Earth Day. It received far more attention than any other event. It was hardly a typical environmental teach-in, but describing it will take a disproportionate amount of this section as it received such a disproportionate amount of coverage.

Six graduate students started the organizing committee, but 350 people attended a planning meeting in October 1969. Triple that number eventually helped make it come off. Planning exposed some rifts in the rank of activists, which to some extent would play out nationwide. Students for a Democratic Society considered most of the featured speakers not liberal enough. One of the principal organizers, horror of horror, was a Republican and Nixon supporter! Black power groups, angry that the plans did not pay sufficient attention to conditions in ghettos, boycotted the teach-in. Activists in antiwar, civil rights, and women's liberation feared that too much attention to the environment would distract too much attention from their issues. On the other hand, most of the students present refused to think of those as separate issues. They also recognized that problems in the environment could not be solved without changes in both the economic system and the choices of individuals.

Although initially planned for two days, the teach-in grew to five days and included 125 different activities. Some were political, with Republican and Socialist student groups offering their perspectives. Some were technical, focused on such issues as how to clean up the Great Lakes or how engineers could prevent pollution. Some were largely entertainment, as when the cast of *Hair* opened the teach-in with a performance of "Age of Aquarius" or speeches by entertainers like Arthur Godfrey and Eddie Albert. Other nationally famous speakers included UAW president Walter Reuther, Ralph Nader, David Brower (founder of Friends of the Earth) and three U.S. senators. Prominent business leaders and scientists also spoke.

Teach-in speakers included representative of several scientific disciplines: biology, ecology, engineering, sociology, public health, and urban studies. Specialists in each branch of science had begun to discover that pollution was more than a nuisance. It threatened the survival of the human race. Representatives of some of the companies most responsible for pollution also spoke, including Detroit Edison, Dow Chemical, and the Ford Motor Company. To those and other companies, interest in the environment must have seemed to come out of nowhere, and they had to address the new public concern. The presence of Dow's president had the additional significance that Dow had become an important target of anti-war activism because of its manufacture of Agent Orange and other chemicals used by the American military in Vietnam. Of course, antiwar activists had their own representatives there. Richard Hatcher, mayor of Gary, Indiana gave the teach-in's closing speech. He was the one of the first black mayors of a major industrial city, and the mostly black residents of Gary especially suffered from the air and water pollution caused by the city's factories. The Michigan teach-in opened to a crowd of 14,000 people. By the end of the week more than 50,000 people had attended.

Barry Commoner was principal speaker at the opening rally. He marveled at the convergence of what had seemed separate issues: not only conservation and environmental health, but the consumer movement, the desire of young people for a more humane lifestyle, problems of urban decay and ghettos, the antiwar movement and other student activism, and the concern of businessmen for what it all meant for industrial profits.

He pointed out that the black student boycott was a mistake. Environmental conditions were worst in the inner city. White suburbanites could leave them behind after work when they returned home, but "the ghetto dweller not only works in a polluted environment, he lives in it" (Carter March 20, 1970).

Commoner insisted that pollution was not a byproduct of recent technological progress or increased factory output, but an intrinsic feature. He recognized that coping with it would come only at the expense of serious economic dislocations, but given the seriousness of the problem, he considered it worth the price. His speech was warmly received by all present except some representatives of Students for a Democratic Society, who considered the invited speakers not sufficiently radical and chose to heckle.

Ralph Nader's speech attacked General Motors and other large industrial companies as "corporate criminals." According to his figures, General Motors plants contributed 45 million tons of air pollution every year. He receive a standing ovation, and teach-in leaders formally requested that Robben Fleming, the university's president, divest its $2.5 million holdings in the company's stock to support the Project on Corporate Responsibility, a project inspired by Nader.

In general students expressed support for a variety of socially disruptive measures including

- Replacing automobiles in urban areas with mass transit
- Less personal consumption generally and a return to simpler lifestyles
- Legalized abortion

⌒ Adoption of tax disincentives and other measures to
   encourage families to have no more than two children as the
   national norm
⌒ Class action suits against polluters
⌒ Requiring recycling or reuse of materials such bottles, cans,
   and paper.
⌒ Campaign support for politicians who would champion such
   ideas

Besides a variety of seminars, workshops, and rallies, teach-in events featured a trial in which an automobile stood accused of pollution. After the guilty verdict, four students with sledgehammers executed the miscreant. Similar mock trials took place on many other campuses nationwide on Earth Day itself.

In his article "Beyond the Teach-In, Commoner provided a sample of plans for various Earth Day teach-ins out of an expected observation at 3000 high schools and 1000 colleges nationwide. The article appeared before any of them actually took place, so he included some events that were under consideration, but not definitely planned (Commoner April 4, 1970).

Assuming it happened according to Commoner's preview, Harvard University's teach-in started the day before Earth Day and featured Michigan speakers Senator Edmund Muskie and Barry Commoner, along with George Wiley, director of the National Welfare Rights Organization. Harvard's own George Wald, a biologist, moderated. Russell Train, chairman of President Nixon's Council on Environmental Controls, was scheduled to speak at the School of Business Administration on Earth Day itself. Students planned anti-SST demonstrations at Logan Airport and contemplated blocking traffic to it on at least one major artery. Pending the cooperation of the weather, they also planned "festivals of life" for various places along the Charles River.

The University of Pennsylvania planned Earth Week, which climaxed on Earth Day. Organizers planned an outdoor rally in Philadelphia's Fairmont Park rain or shine. Senator Muskie and Harvard's Wald were scheduled to travel from Harvard in time to address the crowd. Other announced speakers included beat poet Allen Ginsberg and Ian McHarg, chairman of the university's Department of Landscape, Architecture, and Regional Planning. New York Mayor John Lindsey was scheduled to make a speech at the university.

The University of Texas at Austin, in collaboration with Houston-area classes, planned rallies with both speakers and films that would involve every high school and college in the area. Plans at the University of Wisconsin at Madison were vague, but included somehow liberating Main Street from the automobile. Plans for observance at the University of Chicago included the possibility of a rally downtown at the Civic Center to protest the city's inadequate response to environmental problems. Students at the University of California at Berkeley contemplated dumping garbage on the doorsteps of local polluters. The University of North Carolina at Chapel Hill planned eco-tours of selected polluted areas and "trash-ins" to deposit refuse somewhere—apparently as a clean-up effort and not a protest against particular companies.

The University of Tennessee at Knoxville contemplated a counterpart to Knoxville's "dogwood trail," a "deadwood trail" to polluted areas. Edward Clebsch, an associate professor of botany at Tennessee provided his own preview of plans there. The 20th annual Wildflower Pilgrimage in the Great Smoky Mountains National Park, sponsored by the Botany Department, would be a part of Earth Day plans. There would be a series of lectures jointly sponsored by the Episcopal Center and the Roman Catholic Center. Clebsch and a mathematics professor would lead a four-part workshop to unite representatives of the sciences, social sciences, and arts to discuss the environmental crisis in relation to their own disciplines, dealing with questions of what we had done to the environment; what lifestyles Americans wanted both as individuals, communities, and governments; the price to the environment of those desires, and under what circumstances bargaining becomes impossible (Clebsch 1970).

Southern states generally had weaker environmental movements than the rest of the nation, but hundreds of towns observed Earth Day, albeit less elaborately than the northern and western regions. Birmingham, Alabama used Earth Day as the culmination of a weeklong Right to Live Week. As a steel-producing town, it had bad air quality. People breathed air they could see. Residents accepted that if the air was dirty, it meant people were working and if it was clean the mills were not operating at capacity. The steel mills and coal-dependent Alabama Power enjoyed great political clout. A group called the Greater Birmingham Alliance to Stop Pollution (known as GASP) formed to organize Earth Day. The local medical society and tuberculosis association had long tried to call attention to the air, but the leaders of GASP included two medical doctors who had not grown up in Alabama, Marshall Brewer and Randy Cope. They were not reluctant to challenge industry's political power. Few other Earth Day celebrations focused so completely on a single issue.

The schedule of Right to Live Week included events at clubs and colleges. On the first day, Dr. Cope addressed a woman's club about the recently passed state Air Pollution Control Act, which GASP had labeled a sham and a license to foul the air. Dr. Brewer appealed to churches to devote time to the environment on the Sunday before Earth Day. His speech on Earth Day compared the Earth to the Apollo space program, pointing out that both had limited air and water and that pollution in Birmingham had already resulted in increased respiratory diseases. He urged business leaders to stop leaning on local politicians to refrain from criticizing the Air Pollution Control Act. It was difficult to persuade ordinary citizens that clean air would not require steel workers to lose their jobs, but GASP continued to operate after Earth Day. Under its prodding, the Alabama legislature passed the Clean Air Act in 1971 to replace the Air Pollution Control Act.

Earth Day observations in most communities received only local press coverage, but many took advantage of occasion to point their fingers at local polluters. Automobiles drew disfavor from both students and government officials for causing 60% of the nation's air pollution. Illinois Senator Charles Percy pointed out that the industry spent $1 billion every year for style changes, but only $150 million on anti-pollution research. Even UAW President Walter Reuther declared it asinine for hundreds of thousands of people to commute to work in automobiles and suggested that the auto industry ought to develop mass transit systems.

Unions in general contributed generously to Environmental Action and urged members to participate in Earth Day. Industrial response varied. Some major polluters like Consolidated Edison in New York and Dow Chemical Company sent speakers to meetings on the theory that no one else would have any good word for them. Owners of the Forest Industries building in Washington State set up a temporary forest of potted fir trees to keep demonstrators away and instructed employees in evacuation procedures in case of a riot. Most companies found middle ground between the two extremes, for instance issuing press releases with environmental promises. Handling Earth Day primarily through the public relations department did not sit well even within the business community.

While Earth Day was officially intended as an opportunity to educate the public, not all was peaceful, or for that matter, public. Demonstrators in Boston held a "die-in" by carrying coffins into Logan Airport to protest expansion of the airport and development of the SST. Police arrested 13 people after they ordered demonstrators out and the demonstrators did not leave quickly enough. A housewife in Beesleys Point, New Jersey spent weeks sewing red and black banners with skulls and crossbones and spent much of the night before Earth Day mounting them on dredging equipment that had polluted nearby beaches.

Students in Atlanta dumped cans on the front lawn of Coca Cola's headquarters. People in Clarksburg, West Virginia dumped a ton of litter they had collected from a highway on the courthouse steps. Another man was arrested in Key Biscayne, Florida for violation of local sanitation laws when he protested against thermal pollution of Biscayne Bay by Florida Power and Light Company with a cart of dead fish and a dead octopus. In another dangerous act of wanton criminality, Yippies at Indiana University stole concrete and plugged sewage pipes emptying into the Jordan River

The political and intellectual climate

Democrats controlled both houses of Congress when it passed all of the landmark environmental legislation in the 1970s. Republicans controlled the administration that proposed most of it and oversaw the enabling regulations. In fact, according to the November 9 issue of *Time*, Nixon issued an executive order mandating unleaded fuel in government vehicles after Congress refused his idea to increase taxes on leaded gasoline.

Time devoted articles to specific individuals:
- Illinois Attorney General William Scott (January 5)
- Secretary of Interior Walter Hickel (January 5, March 16)
- Biologist Barry Commoner (February 2)
- Undersecretary of Interior Russell Train (February 9)
- President Richard Nixon (February 23)
- Administrator of the Consumer Protection and Environmental Health Service Charles C. Johnson (March 16)
- Zoologist Kenneth Watt (May 25)
- Secretary of Transportation John Volpe (June 15)

⁓ Kane County, Illinois activist "The Fox" (October 5)
⁓ EPA's first administrator William Ruckelshaus (November 23)
⁓ Rogers Morton, nominated to succeed Hickel as Secretary of Interior (December 14)

What jumps out to me about this list is that every politician or administrator (with the possible exception of Johnson) was a Republican. And every one of them was covered for some positive contribution to environmental protection. Democrats in the House and Senate exercised leadership in environmental issues, but *Time* mentioned them only in passing. One action by Secretary Hickel demonstrates a sort of political division that persists to this day. He promised to issue a permit for the 800-mile Trans-Alaskan Pipeline in order to demonstrate that development and conservation could work together. Conservationists charged that it would probably contaminate the tundra with hot oil.

The somewhat sudden national interest in ecology produced an immediate backlash. Objections came from both sides of the political spectrum.

⁓ The Daughters of the American Revolution, among others, considered the environmental movement just the latest in a series of subversive attempts to undermine American society. As partial proof that it was Communism in disguise, Earth Day coincided with Lenin's birthday.
⁓ Conservatives like Milton Friedman questioned whether it was necessary to cast large corporations as the villains. The real source of most pollution is consumers.
⁓ The director of water resources for Georgia's Union Camp Corp. publicly questioned whether humans would suffer any real harm "if the whooping crane doesn't quite make it."
⁓ Other conservatives fretted that environmental concerns were just another fad that took attention away from more pressing issues of national security.
⁓ On the other hand, several chapters of Students for a Democratic Society took an anti-ecology stand simply because the Nixon administration was pro-ecology. Besides, they said, ecology took attention away from protesting the war in Vietnam.
⁓ Black leaders, including Cleveland's mayor Carl Stokes and Gary, Indiana's mayor Richard Hatcher protested the new fascination with the environment more vocally than anyone

else. The money spent on combating air and water pollution should be spent instead to assist the poor. Hatcher complained that even George Wallace could not do what concern with the environment had done: "distract the nation from the human problems of black and brown Americans" (*Time*, August 3, 1970). He chose to participate in the University of Michigan teach-in despite these reservations.

⁓ When students at San Jose State College in California buried a brand new car to protest environmental damage by automobile, black students picketed, complaining that improving conditions in the ghetto would have been a better way to spend $2,500.

⁓ Frequent suggestions that Americans should consume fewer goods and services likewise irritated blacks.

Immediate outcome—environmental laws and EPA

For at least the next decade, the environment was a safe topic for politicians. No constituency came out against the environment. Earth Day had succeeded in uniting and mobilizing the public around making the nation cleaner and safer by eliminating pollution. Here are important environmental laws passed between the beginning of 1970 and the end of 1980 during the presidencies of Nixon, Ford, and Carter. I have compiled the list from two different websites. Several laws appear on one or the other, but not both. This list is probably not exhaustive, and laws within any specific year are probably not in the order enacted.

⁓ Clean Air Act Amendments (1970)
⁓ National Environmental Policy Act (1970)
⁓ Occupational Safety and Health Act (1970)
⁓ Pollution Prevention Packaging Act (1970)
⁓ Resource Recovery Act (1970)
⁓ Lead-Based Paint Poisoning Prevention Act (1971)
⁓ Coastal Zone Management Act (1972)
⁓ Federal Insecticide, Fungicide, and Rodenticide Act Amendment (1972)
⁓ Marine Mammal Protection Act (1972)
⁓ Marine Protection, Research, and Sanctuaries Act (1972)
⁓ Clean Water Act (1972)
⁓ Endangered Species Act (1973)
⁓ Safe Drinking Water Act (1974)

- Shoreline Erosion Control Demonstration Act (1974)
- Hazardous Materials Transportation Act (1975)
- Federal Land Policy and Management Act (1976)
- Fisheries Conservation and Management Act (Magnuson-Stevens Act) (1976)
- Resource Conservation and Recovery Act (1976)
- Toxic Substances Control Act (1976)
- Clean Water Act Amendments (1977)
- Surface Mining Control and Reclamation Act (1977)
- Uranium Mill-Tailings Radiation Control Act (1978)
- Asbestos School Hazard Detection and Control Act (1980)
- Comprehensive Environmental Response, Compensation, and Liability Act—also known as Superfund (1980)

More environmental laws appeared during this 11-year period than appeared in the 15 years after the end of the Second World War. They deal with both the same issues as earlier laws and new ones. Congress and Presidents Nixon, Ford, and Carter revisited several issues to pass multiple laws. The general consensus in favor of environmental legislation notwithstanding, the issues were difficult both technically and politically.

The Environmental Protection Agency, formed by act of Congress in December 1970, began as a collection of a number of preexisting agencies. In a sense, it can trace its ancestry back to the creation of the U.S. Marine Hospital Service in 1798. Its jurisdiction and mission grew over the years to deal with broader public health issues. Congress changed its name to the U.S. Public Health and Marine Service in 1902 and ten years later deleted "Marine" from the name. The federal regulatory structure began in 1885 with the creation of the Interstate Commerce Commission. Later agencies, including the Food and Drug Administration, began the attempt to define "safe" levels of various pollutants. Eventually, jurisdictions of various agencies not only overlapped, but conflicted, as described in the regulatory situation that led to the "great cranberry scare."

As noted earlier, the common law tradition inherited from the English proved inadequate to deal with the environmental problems that grew more and more serious in the years after the end of the Second World War. Common law lacked sufficient precedents. Conflicting state and local ordinances made it hard for courts to decide how to make proper judgments, especially considering that pollution knows no political boundaries. The New York City metropolitan area intersected with the states of New York,

New Jersey, and Connecticut. Chicago's metropolitan area intersected with Illinois, Indiana, and eventually Wisconsin.

Scientific and technological advances in agriculture, petroleum, plastics, automobiles, aviation, and so on created new substances, which were inflicted on the environment with no thought of their eventual impact. The growing body of environmental law before 1970 dealt with all of these difficulties piecemeal.

The new agency had to balance environmental values against the property rights of individuals and corporations. It had to decide how to interpret scientific findings and use them as the basis of regulations that had to satisfy conflicting interests. Eventually, it had to deal with instances of irrational public hysteria comparable to the cranberry scare.

The EPA became so controversial so quickly that it is now difficult to remember how popular it was in the beginning. William Ruckelshaus, its first director, quickly became the most respected and admired member of the Nixon administration. The landmark environmental legislation of the 1970s quickly brought the conditions that had united the public under control, leaving the more divisive issues for later. By the 1980s, the nation had begun to tire of the sometimes suffocating regulatory structure that had grown over about half a century and demanded deregulation.

Unfortunately, in all the excitement that surrounded the environmental movement and its early victories, the public and government in general did not properly connect the ethos of consumerism with environmental problems. The economy continued to depend on people buying and then discarding vast quantities of not strictly necessary products. Most of the public continued to value their individual rights to convenience and pleasure over the needs of society as a whole. People have continued to point fingers at environmental villains like large corporations and failed to notice the other three fingers pointing back.

What the intellectuals got wrong and still haven't learned

While Republicans provided much of the political leadership behind the legislative and regulatory accomplishments of the first Earth Day, as far as I have been able to find, all of the people most active in writing about environmental issues came from the far left wing of the political spectrum. Today's far left wing environmentalists may have forgotten the abject failure of the predictions made 45 years ago. Or perhaps they only hope the public has. But many of us do remember, and finding written evidence requires only a trip to the library.

Overpopulation and famine

The biggest single issue that united environmental activists was rampant population growth. Paul Ehrlich, author of the bestseller *The Population Bomb*, also wrote numerous magazine articles and appeared frequently on the lecture circuit. Here are some of his predictions:

> So aside from unbreathable air, filthy water, the disappearance of whole species of animals, and a variety of poisons all around us, mankind is also headed for vast famines. Make no mistake about it. (Ehrlich, April 1970)
>
> ********
>
> In our desperate attempts to maintain such a bloated population, we will inevitably do further damage to our environment. Just as inevitably, the human population will complete its outbreak-crash cycle. We've had most of the outbreak—what remains in mainly the crash. For when a biological population outstrips its resources, it inevitably declines rapidly to a very low level—or to extinction. This normally occurs through a dramatic increase in the death rate.
>
> But the human population has some choice left—it can decrease its size either through a rise in the death rate, or through a drop in the birth rate, or some combination of the two. Some increase in the death rate seems unavoidable. (Ehrlich, May 1970)

The most egregiously bad prediction, however, came from Peter A. Gunter, who was completing his first year in the faculty of the Department of Philosophy and Religious Studies at North Texas State University (now the University of North Texas).

> Figuring conservatively, by the year 2000 the world's population will have more than doubled from 3.5 billion persons to 7.2 billion. By the year 2070, one hundred years from now, *every square foot of the earth's surface, deserts,*

rivers, mountains, even oceans, will be built over—just to secure housing space for the planet's twenty to thirty billion people (Gunter 1970, author's emphasis).

A little later, on the same column of the same page, he wrote

Long before the sheer need for space outstrips the capacity of the earth to continue to support additional life, world population will outrun food supplies. Demographers agree almost unanimously on the following grim timetable: by 1975 widespread famines will begin in India; these will spread by 1990 to include all of India, Pakistan, China, the Near East, and Africa. By the year 2000, or conceivably sooner, South and Central America will exist under famine conditions.

Why did he not stop to think about the sheer impossibility of both predictions occurring? How could the population double in 30 years while at the same time most of the entire world would have been in famine? The only way to account for such drivel appearing in print is editorial irresponsibility, probably combined with excessive awe of the author's academic credentials. Gunter hedged another wild prediction writing, "if present trends continue." But that's the whole problem with all of the predictions of looming disaster. Present trends never continue. The mistaken notion that somehow they will has driven the rhetoric of overpopulation for centuries. Thomas Malthus was wrong in 1798. Ehrlich, Gunter, and many others were wrong in 1970.

At the very time Ehrlich warned that India could never be self-sufficient in food, Norman Borlaug had already begun to make India self sufficient in food. Borlaug himself warned about the dangers of population growth. But instead of wringing his hands and waiting for mass starvation, he found ways to increase food supply. He won the Nobel Peace Prize in 1970 for his efforts. Ehrlich remains better known than Borlaug today, mostly because Borlaug spent so much time in the field and was not a prolific, self-promoting author. Since Borlaug is so little known today, a little background is necessary in order to understand his achievement.

Borlaug was born in Cresco, Iowa on March 25, 1914. He entered the University of Minnesota as a freshman in 1933 and found living conditions shocking. He had known hunger growing up, but was not used to seeing homeless grown men and whole homeless families begging for change and food. Eventually he earned a degree in forest management, but could not get a job. So he started graduate work in plant pathology, studying rust, a fungus that kills many different crops.

The Depression coincided with some of the worst drought conditions in American history. As crops withered and died, nothing held the soil in place. The American Midwest became the Dust Bowl. Before the late 1930s, the cornfields produced only 30 bushels per acre, but Iowa farmers had begun developing new hybrid corn and using fertilizers. As a result, as Borlaug observed first hand, they boosted yields to an average of 75 bushels of corn per acre. The farms that most systematically used the new technology suffered less from Dust Bowl conditions.

These observations caused him to dedicate his life to taking high-yield farming to the rest of the world in order to reduce crop failures and save lives. In 1943 the Rockefeller Foundation established what eventually became the International Maize and Wheat Center in Mexico. Borlaug became its director. He and his team introduced important innovations:

- They crossbred thousands of wheat varieties from all over the world and produced seeds that are resistant to rust. Yields of wheat increased 20-40% as a result.
- They developed dwarf wheat, which increased yields even more. Conventional tall wheat must expend energy to grow long stalks, so shorter wheat can expend more on growing edible grain. And the grain does not cause the stalk to bend under the weight of ripe wheat. Tall wheat sometimes even bent to the ground and became unharvestable.
- They pioneered a technique called shuttle breeding, growing and harvesting two crops a year in two different regions of Mexico instead of one. Being able to test two generations of wheat every year cut the time required to develop his new seeds in half. In addition, growing test crops in different regions produced seeds that could grow in many latitudes, altitudes, and soil types.

Much of the world now depends on dwarf wheat for survival. In 1950, farmers worldwide harvested 692 million tons of grain for 2.2 billion people. In 1992 they grew 1.9 billion tons of grain for 5.6 billion people. By that time, the world had 2.2 times as many people, but produced 2.8 times as much grain—on about the same acreage.

India in the mid-1960s faced disaster. Its founding Prime Minister, Jawaharlal Nehru, died in 1964, and India had not yet demonstrated that it could develop stable democratic government and peaceful political succession. Nehru had focused so much of his attention on developing heavy industry that his government neglected agriculture. The new Prime Minister had to deal with droughts in both 1966 and 1967, which threatened India with massive famine. India's minister of Food and Agriculture learned of Borlaug's work in Mexico and sought his help in India. The Indian government imported 16,000 metric tons of his dwarf wheat seeds.

Borlaug went there to lead an effort to teach Indian and Pakistani farmers how to cultivate it properly. He faced more difficulties there than he had in Mexico, not the least of which is that war broke out between India and Pakistan shortly after he arrived. Sometimes he had to teach farmers how to plant and care for the new seeds while artillery flashed within sight. Far from experiencing mass starvation, Pakistan became self-sufficient in wheat production by 1968. India followed within a few years, becoming self-sufficient in all cereal grains by 1974. Food production in both countries has grown faster than the population.

Unfortunately, it appears that Earth Day speakers either did not know of Borlaug's achievements or deliberately ignored them to keep the public from finding out. I find no voice raised to inform Ehrlich and his ilk that the facts on the ground in India and Pakistan completely destroyed their entire case.

Although Barry Commoner (Commoner, April 4, 1970) was alarmed at the rapid growth in population in underdeveloped parts of the world, he pointed out that the pollution problem was not a consequence of excess population. In particular, the calls for zero growth in the American population completely missed the point. In the twenty years after the end of the Second World War the "baby boom" years, the U.S. population increased by 43%, a large increase. But use of electric power had increased by almost 400%. Use of pesticides had increased more than 500%, and use of fertilizer by nearly 700%. Consumption, not population, drove American environmental problems. Nevertheless, the concept of zero population growth and limiting families to two children caught on to the extent that Lee DuBridge, President Nixon's science advisor, and Health, Education, and Welfare Secretary Robert H. Finch both endorsed it publicly.

The coming ice age

Overpopulation and famine have almost disappeared from the shrill warnings of looming catastrophe, but the leading speakers and writers of the day made another colossal blunder that directly explains why the majority of Americans today pay no attention to climate change rhetoric. Al Gore deliberately picked one of the hottest days of summer to announce his crusade against global warming. The climate is not at all the same thing as the weather—a fact that is all too conveniently forgotten by people on both sides of the argument.

Ehrlich wrote

... the details of the generation of weather are complex and poorly understood. It is possible that an overall rise in temperature of a few degrees could produce a much *colder* climate in many localities, caused by changes in the speed or direction of circulation bringing more cold air from polar regions...

Man's activities and construction also have significant local effects on weather, but it is his influence on large-scale climatic change that is of greatest concern, for there can be little doubt that such change has been accelerated on a global basis with almost complete disregard for possible consequences. Some of the changes which have been predicted would be cataclysmic—slippage of the Antarctic ice cap, causing tidal waves which would wipe out most of humanity; or the sudden onset of a new ice age (Ehrlich May 1970).

Ehrlich was not alone. Unfortunately, I have been unable to trace some of the other predictions I have read about. One web site —which offers as a source only another very poorly documented website quotes Kenneth Watt, identified there only as an ecologist.

The world has been chilling sharply for about twenty years. If present trends continue, the world will be about four degrees colder for the global mean temperature in 1990, but eleven degrees colder in the year 2000. This is about twice what it would take to put us into an ice age.

Note once again the phrase, "if present trends continue."

At the same time alarmist amateurs churned out articles for the mass media, Eugene K. Peterson, Chief of the Division of Basin Studies with the Bureau of Land Management and therefore a real climate scientist, published a lucid explanation in a scientific journal of the state of the climate and what conditions would cause either warming or cooling (Peterson, Spring 1970). At the time, oxygen made about 21% of the atmosphere and carbon dioxide about 0.032%. The ratio between the two was 650 to 1. Peterson was more concerned about changes to that ratio than either radioactivity or smog. Atmospheric carbon dioxide and worldwide mean temperatures had been increasing since 1860. American geologist T. C. Chamberlain first proposed the possibility that release of carbon dioxide from burning fossil fuels could increase worldwide temperatures. Calculations made in 1967 indicated that a doubling of carbon dioxide would raise surface temperatures 4.25 degrees F, all else being equal. . Carbon dioxide in the atmosphere increased by 1.13% or 3.7 parts per million between 1958 to 1962, a figure that represents half of the carbon dioxide that resulted from burning fossil fuels. The oceans apparently absorbed the rest.

Carbon dioxide is among the so-called greenhouse gases that insulate the atmosphere, but increased carbon dioxide by itself does not necessarily mean that it will warm the earth. There are too many complex relationships to study and too many unknown factors. Particulates in the atmosphere tend to reduce temperatures. Increased temperatures reduce how much carbon dioxide the oceans can dissolve, and increase the amount of it the oceans would release into the atmosphere and therefore accelerate the rate of warming. A similar multiplier would work the other direction in the case of decreased temperatures.

Peterson cited J. M. Mitchell of the Environmental Science Services Administration, who determined that between 1885 and 1940, average mean temperatures rose 0.9 degrees F, and the rise was not uniform all over the globe. It was greatest between 40 and 70 degrees north latitude. Average winter temperatures rose 2.8 degrees F there. Northern hemisphere temperatures rose about 3.6 degrees. Additional warming occurred in northern Europe and North America between 1940 and 1960, but mean average temperatures dropped 0.2 degrees worldwide. According to pre-liminary indications, the cooling trend had continued since 1960. Mitchell noted a consistent tendency for average temperatures to drop about 0.1 degrees in the five years after major volcanic eruptions. The cooling observed during the 1950s could possibly be attributed to eruptions in Alaska (1953) and Kamchatka, USSR (1956).

Climate has been changing either slowly or rapidly for much longer than the human race has existed. Ice age alarmists apparently noticed a drop in average mean temperature over the previous 30 years and did not bother to investigate what caused the trend or whether it was likely to continue. Today's global warming alarmists are more nearly correct about longer-term climate trends, but no more careful to take careful note of all the complex variables. The so-called Little Ice Age began in about 1300. Various writers estimate that it ended around 1800 or 1900. Five or six hundred years before the Little Ice Age, the climate was warmer than it is now. Periodic warming or cooling before the Industrial Revolution clearly owed nothing to human activity. If the Little Ice Age ended closer to 1800, burning of fossil fuels and the resulting increase in carbon dioxide could not have caused it, but certainly can increase a warming trend that would be happening anyway. The closer to 1900 the Little Ice Age ended, the more likely industrial activity played a role. Meanwhile, recent studies of Greenland's ice sheet has determined that human activity (metallurgy, blacksmiths, and rice farming) as long ago as ancient Rome and the Han Dynasty in China contributed to increased atmospheric methane, another greenhouse gas (Stromberg 2013).

There is no question that our modern industrial lifestyle has affected both the weather and the climate. The notion that *only* modern industrial lifestyle has affected climate is absurd.

Attacks on mainstream society

The loudest voices proclaiming that human activity directly causes climate change often seem to have favored a radical, government-mandated redistribution of wealth. If a history of bad predictions is not enough reason why climate change rhetoric does not resonate, the mindless attacks on the profit motive provide another. But that, too, is leftover from 1970s environmental rhetoric. The population alarmists favored anything that would lead to a decrease in the American population (as well as everywhere else).

As much as many authors appealed to democracy, others of them could not have cared less what the public thought. Most chilling, here is an observation by Luther Gerlach in his review of two books, *Ecotactics: The Sierra Club Handbook for Environmental Activists* and The *Environmental Handbook.*

> For instance, Garrett Hardin argues that man will not be motivated to decrease environmental despoliation simply by appealing to his conscience or warning him of impending disaster . . . Hardin explains that instead man *must be*

coerced by official restrictions if he is to be restrained from exploiting his environment to its death" – emphasis added

I wonder if that sentiment still resides in some advocates of "progressive" politics, with its use of courts to force legal changes opposed by mainstream Americans, and hateful rhetoric to demonize anyone who does not accept their viewpoint. During the 1970s, Norman Borlaug's success in eliminating mass starvation in Mexico, India, and Pakistan came to environmental extremists' attention at about the time he began to work in Africa. They began to threaten Borlaug's main sources of funding and frightened them into withdrawing support. Africa remains the only continent where widespread starvation still exists. Unstable governments probably bear most of the responsibility, but did the people who hampered Borlaug's work prefer to starve people to death rather than renounce their fealty to Ehrlich's population hoax and feed them?

Progressive rhetoric has also long voiced opposition to traditional moral values. Margaret Sanger, founder of Planned Parenthood, championed birth control and abortion in order to exterminate black people and other undesirables. Like Hardin, she favored government coercion and wanted to make parents obtain permission from the government to have children. When progressives rejected Sanger's racism and supported the Civil Rights movement, the phony population scare and zero growth movement began to demand abortion to eliminate what Ehrlich called "people pollution." No demand for abortion was complete without an explicit attack on Christianity:

> And certainly abortion laws have to be changed. I don't mean "liberalized." I mean changed. Women have to be able to obtain easy, inexpensive, and safe abortions, and the social stigma should be removed from doing so (Ehrlich April 1970).

Later in the same interview:

> We have a very confused sense of morality in this country, you know . . . They [opponents of American aid to a sterilization program in India] get all worked up over the morality of legalizing abortions, but they go about their business while hundreds of thousands of people are dying in Southeast Asia . . ."

Ehrlich more explicitly challenged American religion in another article

> A rapid change in human attitudes will be necessary—changes in attitudes about such fundamental things as reproduction, competition, and economic growth. The Judeo-Christian idea of man dominating nature must be replaced by the goal of living in harmony with nature (Ehrlich May 1970).

He was not alone in this critique.

> In this article it is not possible to consider in depth just what this new mind-set will involve. A few suggestions however, will suffice to show the kind of transformation of our long-cherished economic and theological assumptions that is called for. The official position of the Roman Catholic Church on birth control is often cited by environmentalists as a prime example of backward thinking in a time of radical change (Gunter 1970).

Thus did left-wingers hijack the environmental movement and propose to solve environmental problems at the expense of killing Africans, the unborn, and other helpless people. We have plenty of unsolved environmental problems left over from the 1970s. We also have some new ones. Maybe we would make more progress on the environment if we did not also have so much left over empty fear mongering and other ideological excesses.

What Earth Day Leaders forgot

I do not remember an Earth Day teach-in at my university. My overly ambitious course load kept me away from any kind of special event until the Kent State massacre in May, for which the university suspended classes for a week. But I do remember that my friends and I got really excited about the environment. At least I managed to keep reading voraciously in addition to class work. I hungered to learn whatever I could. Unfortunately, the Earth Day organizers had a big blind spot. They limited their plans to education and political action and completely failed to consider what else they could encourage ordinary citizens to do with their lives.

Besides reading and some kind of political action, I had no idea what to do about it. Besides recycling, I still had little enough idea until a started serving on a university sustainability committee just a few years ago. I will later share some of what I learned, but here I will examine what environmental leaders wrote in 1970. Shortly after Earth Day concluded, an assessment of its impact, along with speculation about what might happen next, appeared in the journal *Science*. It is the best statement I have found of what people were expected to do.

Earth Day was a start, and may have been the launching date of a lasting crusade. But what will follow? The days following religious revivals and old-fashioned Fourth of July celebrations saw many backsliders and much business as usual. Earth Day, too, may be forgotten, or ears may be dulled by overexposure and people may quit listening to the Earth Day message.

No single event will keep people listening, and the tactics that gave Earth Day its impact will wear out too soon. The Sierra Club announced *Ecotactics,* its handbook for environmental activists, as dealing with "teach-ins, attacks on giant industry pollution practices, community concern, boycotts . . . " These activities are calculated to rouse excitement, but they are not a long-range strategy for maintaining widespread concern for environmental problems or for understanding the management alternatives (Wolfle 1970).

While I certainly have not uncovered everything published in 1970, or even most of it, about Earth Day, Wolfle is the almost the only author I found who recognized the shortcomings of organized political action, although one article quoted Undersecretary of Interior Russell Train. Although he said he was delighted to see so much energy channeled into environmental law, he warned, "We can't govern by protest, demonstration, and litigation" (Main 1970).

I have already quoted a review of a book by Garrett Hardin, who wrote that the government must coerce people into taking acceptable (to him) environmental action. Other authors who mentioned ordinary citizens at all did not share Hardin's cynicism, but also lacked Wolfle's insight. Here is an article by a professor of religious studies at North Texas State University:

Concerning these increasingly obvious—and more and more ominous—problems, more is being said and written, almost daily. Unfortunately, however, very little is being done about them. Hard-pressed conservationists, frightened population experts, exasperated scientists have managed, in part, to gain the attention of the "man in the street." But both government and industry have been slow to act, and, indeed, have continued in many cases to act as if there were no real problem at all. – (Gunter 1970).

But exactly what did Gunter think the "man in the street" should do once all the frightened "experts" got his attention? In several articles by Ehrlich, I found only this recommendation:

> People have got to demand and make sure they receive an environmental bill of rights that the Government is forced to protect. (Ehrlich April 1970).

Chapter 3 Mixed Longer Term Results of Earth Day

American society has a short attention span and a short memory. From 1945, when most of the public and most of the federal government were apathetic about the environment, until the end of the Ford administration, the environmental movement grew in strength and influence. President Carter had no less commitment to the environment, but was much less successful than his predecessors in accomplishing his legislative goals. Meanwhile, the business community had started to lose enthusiasm for new environmental laws and regulations. Carter ordered solar panels installed for the White House. President Reagan ordered them removed. Deregulation became the order of the day.

Enactment of new federal environmental legislation continued, but the rate slowed noticeably after 1980. The following list comes from the same two web sites as the list in Chapter 2 with the same caveat. Each list contains laws not in the other, and the laws for any given year are probably not listed in the order passed.

- Nuclear Waste Policy Act (1982)
- Asbestos School Hazard Abatement Act (1984)
- Asbestos Hazard Emergency Response Act (1986)
- Emergency Planning and Community Right to Know Act (1986)
- Superfund Amendments and Reauthorization Act (1986)
- Clean Water Act Amendments (1987)
- Indoor Radon Abatement Act (1988)
- Lead Contamination Control Act (1988)
- Medical Waste Tracking Act (1988)
- Ocean Dumping Ban Act (1988)
- Clean Air Act Amendments (1990)
- Clean Water Act Amendments (1990)
- National Environmental Education Act (1990)
- Oil Pollution Control Act (1990)
- Pollution Prevention Act (1990)
- Food Quality Protection Act (1996)
- Chemical Safety Information, Site Security and Fuels Regulatory Relief Act (1999)

Problems solved since 1970, at least partially

In celebration of its 40th anniversary, the EPA released statistics that showed its effectiveness. Unfortunately, the numbers rarely compare 1970 and 2010 directly. Recycling went from negligible in 1970 to 10% of trash in 1980 to 33% of trash in 2008. From the passage of the Superfund Act of 1980 to 2010, the EPA cleaned 67% of contaminated sites. Brownfield sites thereby became available for development of neighborhoods and businesses. The cleanup put 3,300 Americans to work.

A 60% reduction in air pollutants occurred between the 1970 amendments to the Clean Air Act and 2010. Smog, acid rain, and lead poisoning are less serious problems than before. New technologies like smokestack scrubbers and catalytic converters helped. Cars were 98% cleaner in the 2009 or 2010 model year than in 1970. Improvements in air quality decreased premature death, childhood respiratory illnesses, chronic bronchitis, asthma, heart disease, and losses in children's IQ from lead poisoning.

Half of the lakes had less nutrient concentration (green sludge) and a quarter demonstrated improved trophic levels (the position organisms occupy in a food chain) from the 1970s to 2007. More than 2,000 bodies of water considered impaired as recently as 2002 met water quality standards by 2010. As noted in chapter 1, many municipal water supplies presented public health hazards in 1970. By 1993, 70% of Americans received water that met health standards, a percentage that increased to 92% in 2008. From 1968 to 2008, publicly-owned wastewater treatment plants served 60% more Americans.

The auto industry in general took on the role of environmental villain, but *Look* regarded Henry Ford II as one of the "good guys." It invited him to write for a section of its coverage called "Five Who Care" (Shepherd April 21, 1970). It is instructive to compare the EPA's claims about the improvements to automobiles with Ford's article. He called the environmental crisis industry's biggest issue, but noted that industry could not be environmentally responsible without government regulations. Otherwise the polluters would have lower costs and higher profits than their more responsible competitors. He challenged the idea that pollution from cars was getting worse and that neither industry nor government was doing anything about it. California's vehicle emission standards led to an 80% reduction in hydrocarbons and a 70% reduction of carbon monoxide in less than 10 years. One 1950 car emitted five times as much hydrocarbon as five 1970 cars. California had new standards in the works to control oxides of nitrogen. By 1975, Ford predicted, internal combustion engines would be virtually emission-free.

Ford Motor Company spent $66 million over ten years to reduce pollution from the manufacturing process and planned to spend $60 million more in 1970-71. One of its contractors devised a way that Ford hoped would reduce particulate discharges from its coke ovens by 85%. He did not intend for his description of improvements to deny the need for more progress and acknowledged that further progress would be expensive, but he considered the need to control pollution urgent. Leaving aside the question of what percentage of the company's spending the outlays for pollution control represented vis a vis the advertising budget, his prediction of its quick success did not come to pass. Even if the EPA's claims about improvements in emissions are completely correct, automobile exhaust continues to be an environmental hazard.

Much of Lake Erie had been declared dead by 1970, killed by algae blooms that thrived on phosphates and other nutrients in sewage and agricultural run-off. The May 4 issue of *Time* mentions a different pollutant in the Great Lakes: mercury. When tests showed that fish in Lake Saint Claire had fourteen times the maximum level of mercury considered safe for humans to eat, Secretary of the Interior Walter Hickel ordered a federal investigation of all lethal substances discharged into the Great Lakes. The state of Michigan ordered the closure of a Wyandotte Chemicals plant. Other states, as well as Ontario, Canada likewise took vigorous action. The water of the Great Lakes is hardly pristine today, but people can eat the fish. The dead spot in Lake Erie long ago came back to life. Unfortunately, that does not mean that we can see algae blooms in our rearview mirror. They are just smaller and more localized, like the one that contaminated drinking water in Toledo, Ohio in August 2014.

Municipal tap water is no longer a public health menace, as it was in some places in 1970. Some people today are suspicious of tap water, but thanks to the Safe Drinking Water Act municipal water supplies are safe to drink everywhere—provided, of course, no company has befouled a river with a chemical spill.

Housewives regularly polluted rivers and groundwater every time they did laundry. Available detergents relied on phosphates and were not biodegradable. In streams, algae blooms killed fish. In municipalities that depended on well water and septic tanks, like Suffolk County on Long Island, tap water came out foamy and obnoxious smelling. The November 23 issue of *Time* reported that Suffolk County passed an ordinance to ban the sale of detergents, with hefty fines and possible jail time for stores that did not comply. Nothing in the ordinance kept people from going to another county to buy detergent. Fortunately the chemicals and manufacturing techniques that caused the problems have long been illegal.

Pesticides have improved since 1970, but pesticide resistance is still a problem. DDT and readily available substitutes were all part of the same family of chemicals, organophosphates. They were non-selective fumigants. That is, they were applied as a toxic gas that killed both undesirable and desirable insects—not to mention birds, mammals, and fish. Today the pesticide industry has developed a wide array of chemical classes. Although herbicides did not receive nearly as much attention as insecticides, they presented similar problems, particularly the development of resistance. Some current pesticides are highly selective, although none is yet selective enough to kill only a single species. Some kill insects or weeds on contact. Some work systemically; pests absorb them, and they move within the organism and cause death. Systemic insecticides can be applied to the soil, to plants, or to animals. The insects absorb them by, for example, eating the treated plants or sucking the blood of treated animals.

In principal, the variety of chemical classes guards against resistance development. In practice, pests will very likely develop resistance eventually, anyway. Users can help delay the development of resistance by rotating among the various chemical classes of pesticides and being careful to use them according to directions. Perhaps even more important than availability of a wider variety of chemicals, scientists have developed non-chemical means of pest control, such as disruption of mating with pheromones and encouraging pests' natural enemies. Certain insects eat other insects. Birds eat insects. Farmers and gardeners are beginning to learn how to attract them.

Less of a crisis than an irritant, dog poop made it into the July 20 issue of *Time*. Some people wanted to ban large dogs from big cities! Nowadays most dog owners know to pick up after their pets. Piles of poop are still irritating, but no longer newsworthy.

Problems not solved

Barry Commoner provided an excellent overview of the underlying scientific principles of ecology as understood in 1970:

> All living things including man, and all human activities on the surface of the earth, including all of our technology, industry, and agriculture, are dependent on the great interwoven cyclical process followed by the four elements that make up the major portion of living things and the environment: carbon, oxygen, hydrogen, and nitrogen. All of these cycles are driven by the action of living things: green plants convert carbon dioxide into food, fiber, and fuel; and the same time they produce oxygen so that the total oxygen in our atmosphere is the product of plant activity. Plants also convert inorganic nutrients into foodstuffs. Animals, basically, live on plant-produced food; in turn they regenerate the inorganic materials—carbon dioxide, nitrates, and phosphates—which must support plant life. Also involved are myriads of microorganisms in the soil and water. Altogether this vast web of biological interactions generates the very physical system in which we live: the soil and the air. It maintains the purity of surface waters and by governing the movement of water in the in the soil and its evaporation into the air regulates the weather. This is the environment. It is a place created by living things, maintained by living things, and through the marvelous reciprocities of biological evolution is essential to the support of living things.
>
> The city clearly illustrates our dependence on the environment for it is sustained by essential links to a number of ecological systems. Thus the purity of the water which is delivered to the city dweller is achieved by biological processes in some distant waterway. In thru, the city releases its sewage wastes to nearby waterways, imposing on their self-cleansing biological systems a strain which must be overcome if local beaches are to be usable and if downstream communities are to have pure water for their own needs. The city must have air to support its life; but it discharges massive wastes into it, so that the purity of the air becomes,

again, dependent on natural processes in the weather system. Similarly, the city is linked to the land by its requirements for food, as well as water. Organic wastes, such as garbage, which in nature sustain the fertility of the soil, are carelessly thrust back into the environment by the city as landfill or through incineration. And the city has its own internal ecological problems; rats and other vermin live on waste, and in their proliferation contribute to human misery (Commoner April 1970).

The oil spill in Santa Barbara, California in 1969 continued to make news into 1970. *Time* ran stories about it in the February 9 and June 22 issues. Other oil related problems occurred before Santa Barbara dropped out of the news cycle. Due to the negligence of the Chevron Oil Co., a dozen oil wells caught fire and burned for a month. The names of people and companies in the news have changed since 1970. Locations have changed. Our large corporations still have not learned to handle oil safely. Getting it right most of the time is not good enough. Oil spills (and spills of other hazardous materials) still regularly occur. At least one advance in understanding seems permanent. A sentence in the March 23 issue of *Time* about the Chevron disaster would never appear in a news report these days: "Fortunately the slicks blew out to sea." Now we know that oil damages more than beaches.

Other pollution issues made the news all year. The Nixon administration ordered all federal facilities to end pollution, or at least have plans in progress by 1972. The state of California decided not to wait and sued Ft. Ord for dumping sewage into Monterrey Bay (March 16). At the beginning of the year, mercury in water had seemed a problem limited to the Great Lakes. Then it was found in 33 states after 20 years of companies dumping it into various waterways (September 28). As industrial agriculture supplanted the traditional family farm, farm animals were confined to smaller and smaller spaces. The ground could no longer process the wastes. Already, organic wastes from feedlots exceeded the sewage created by the entire population of the United States. Most suggestions for dealing with this fairly new problem were impractical (September 14).

More practical solutions are in sight, if not yet implemented. Successful pilot programs to use manure as a resource—mostly for producing electricity or natural gas—have been announced in the press for years, and yet farmers deal with it mostly by collecting it in foul-smelling and unsanitary lagoons. Manure is the very best fertilizer for crops, but petrochemicals continue to provide for the bulk of fertilizer actually used. The addition of ethanol to gasoline first happened as a result of the huge surpluses of corn that Vance Packard pointed out. The federal government subsidizes it substantially. More recently, we find that American farmers no longer produce surpluses. They could export more corn for food if they were not required to sell it for the manufacture of ethanol. And once a subsidy starts, unless it has a specific and firm sunset date, it becomes politically impossible to halt it even after the reason for it no longer exists.

Abundant water never seems to be where people want it to be. The March 23 and July 6 issues of *Time* covered news of a massive and controversial project to move water from northern California to southern California. The issue still causes friction between the two parts of the state. No technology exists that can move water from areas experiencing massive flooding to areas experiencing severe to extraordinary drought. At least in part, that is because in many parts of the country an area that suffers flood one year is likely to face drought later, sometimes as soon as the following year.

Conservation vs development

As early as the first conservationist battles against dam building, we have been embroiled in debates, never likely to end, on how to handle the often-conflicting values of development and environmental preservation. In Florida, Miami-Dade County wanted to build the world's largest airport near Everglades National Park, one that could accommodate SST flights. Environmentalists began to fight the plan immediately, and in January 1970 the Nixon administration pressured the airport authority to look for another site within 6 months, but one runway had already been built. Environmentalists also prevented completion of the Cross Florida Barge Canal, but again after construction had begun. Those two projects only begin to describe environmental controversy in Florida alone that year.

Vermont's governor complained, "The worse pollution becomes in New York and Boston, the more people will think about moving to the country" (*Time* November 9, 1970). Meanwhile, Vermont's own clean air was under threat from slipshod real estate development and the state's attempt to attract industry. State laws to regulate water pollution came to nothing when the environmental control board and the governor ruled in favor of a new tissue paper manufacturing plant and against the recommendation of a district environmental commission. The same issue of *Time* also mentions a group in Arizona that called itself "Town Hall," which was trying to put a halt to that state's attempts to attract new residents. Part of its mission was to teach Arizonans that rampant growth is not the same thing as progress. The whole country still needs to learn that.

The federal government owned a hodgepodge of 755 million acres of land, including national forests operated by the Department of Agriculture, creating unavoidable tension between logging and mining interests on the one hand and recreational interests on the other. The Public Land Law Review Commission finished six years of work by releasing a report that was supposed to have forged a compromise. Its overwhelmingly commercial tone especially displeased environmentalists. The Nixon administration endorsed part of it. Alaska chose to develop north shore oil fields that turned it from a pauper state to a prosperous one. The drilling and pipeline remain controversial to this day.

The March 23 issue of *Time* noted that a scheme to irrigate Death Valley would "soon test man's reverence for life," because it would mean the extinction of the amazing but economically useless Death Valley pupfish. Thereafter, environmentalists regularly made the news trying to block developments and large-scale engineering projects in order to save some obscure species from extinction. We do not hear so much about that issue anymore, not because wildlife diversity has ceased to matter, but because the tactics did not work and turned too many people against the whole idea of protecting the environment. Man's reverence for life has, on the whole, passed the test, but we still have no consensus when it comes to the issue of preservation versus development.

I have been very critical of Ehrlich for his overheated fear-mongering about overpopulation. But it is hard to find fault with his article about over-fishing. At the time, Americans seemed to welcome the challenge of feeding the whole world. As part of the effort, many voices touted the ocean as a major new source of food for a hungry world. Ehrlich countered that it would require vastly increasing the amount of seafood harvested annually.

But two problems stand between man and the future achievement of that seventy million or more tons of yield. The first is overexploitation, the second is oceanic pollution.

The story of the whale fisheries serves as a model of overexploitation (Ehrlich and Ehrlich, April 4, 1970).

Two articles from *Time* make similar points:

- Japanese and Russians had killed so many whales that the population of some species had become dangerously low. The International Whaling Commission declined to lower the allowable quotas (July 20).
- Besides documenting how polluted the oceans had become, Jacques Yves Cousteau warned about the brutal effects of modern fishing techniques. Eggs and larvae got scooped up along with the fish and other seafood (September 28).

Hunting whales has since been greatly reduced. Only 1,000 were killed in 2012 as opposed to the 57,891 Ehrlich reported for 1966. Unfortunately, according to the *New York Times*, pollution now kills more whales annually than hunting. As far as over-exploitation of fish for human food is concerned, when is the last time orange roughy appeared on a restaurant menu? It was severely overfished. Even the cod off the New England coast that once seemed limitless have been reduced dramatically. In 1970, it was sardines that seemed unlimited. Hedgpeth noted that California fisheries had 20-40 years advance warning of the danger of overfishing sardines. They continued harvesting sardines at the same rate until the predictions came true (Hedgpeth, Spring 1970). Besides dangerously reducing populations of fish used for food, modern fishing methods result in "bycatch," that is, what is caught unintentionally. Bycatch includes undersized juveniles of the target species, undesirable fish species, whatever birds, sea turtles, etc. that get swept up with everything else. Most of it must simply be discarded.

Proper use of technology

After the quotation at the head of this section, Commoner went on to assert that the cause of modern environmental problems was not inadequate technology, but the very success of our technology. Environmentalists not infrequently conclude that if technology is the problem, then we must stop using it. It seems to me more to the point that the problem is not so much technology itself, but the kind of intellectual laziness that encourages us to develop technology and deploy it without exploring possible consequences. We compound an environmental problem when we invent new technologies to solve it, still without inadequate investigation of how the original problems arose in the first place. And regardless of how well technology is designed to work with nature instead of against it, momentary carelessness in applying it continues to have long-term catastrophic results.

Lack of foresight probably remains the most serious unsolved problem, and it appears to be hardwired into human nature. For example manufacturers of detergents before Earth Day did not test their formulas to ensure environmental safety. Therefore they did not know that their formula would kill fish in rivers and lakes and even contribute to the death of Lake Erie. Whoever devised the plan of spraying DDT everywhere to eradicate insect pests did not know that the chemical would wreak such ecological havoc while the insects developed immunity to it. The Pentagon did not know, as it began to make national defense dependent on nuclear weapons, that fallout from atomic tests would endanger all life forms anywhere the radioactive clouds drifted.

They did not know because they did not think to investigate beforehand. And after the problems emerged, the first tendency of industry in each case was to deny responsibility. The legal bullying Rachel Carson and her publishers suffered may have been the first time industry chose to resort to intimidation, ridicule, scare tactics, and using campaign contributions to tie the hands of lawmakers. It certainly has not been the last. Some industries eventually recognize that their products or corporate practices cause some kind of harm and take steps to correct the situation. Others never do and continue punish anyone who opposes them.

We are not curious enough before devising environmental mitigation plans, either. Soot and fly ash from smokestacks was hardly a new problem after the Second World War. It had existed as long as smoke stacks had. Coal had been the primary culprit since the start of the Industrial Revolution. Soot and ash first became sufficiently objectionable for public protest after the war. Burning coal produces two kinds of ash. Bottom ash remains in the chimney. Fly ash exits through the smoke stack and drifts.

The larger particles of fly ash from coal-burning power plants fell on surrounding neighborhoods, including laundry drying on clotheslines. Smaller particles remained in the atmosphere and contributed to smog. Clean air legislation of the 1970s mandated scrubbers to keep fly ash out of the air. As much as industry fought the requirement, some smokestacks were equipped with scrubbers as early as the late 1940s. Burning coal produced just as much ash as before, but it remained on site and became the owners' waste disposal problem. Simply piling ash somewhere would not solve it. Whether at the top of a chimney or at ground level, fly ash is very light; the wind would blow it away.

The question became how to dispose of it. Collecting the ash in deep pits and mixing it with water to prevent it from blowing away became the state of the art. To the best of my knowledge, all ash ponds were built immediately adjacent to a lake or river. No one knew or thought of investigating that without liners, chemicals in the pits would leach into groundwater. As ash settled to the bottom of the pits, it became necessary, or at least expedient, to discharge relatively clean water from the top of the pit into nearby lakes or streams. Sometimes, with EPA approval and oversight, utilities released ash itself. No one knew or thought of investigating that the concentration of heavy metals would deform fish and make it impossible for them to reproduce—quite apart from rendering them unfit to eat.

Dams separate the ash pits from adjacent rivers. Surely engineers and regulators knew that dams can fail if not properly maintained. Unfortunately no one thought about the consequences of coal ash in a waterway until December 22, 2008, when a dam failed at a Tennessee Valley Authority plant at Kingston, Tennessee. The collapse suddenly released 5.4 million cubic yards of coal ash into the Emory and Clinch Rivers and onto 300 acres of land. On such occasions, engineers, politicians, and others promise a full investigation and appropriate changes to make sure that nothing of the kind ever happens again. But it always does.

In the 1940s, someone at the Dan River Steam Plant in Eden, North Carolina noticed that rainwater collected in a depression on the other side of the ash pit from the river. A heavy storm could cause enough clean water to pour into the pit that it would overtop the dam, so Duke Power, the owner, decided to build a drainage pipe by tunneling under the pit. No other ash pit anywhere sits atop a drainage pipe. That bit of cleverness was just the first of a number of bad decisions that led to disaster when the pipe collapsed on February 2, 2014 and released coal ash into the river. Consider:

⁓ The state of the art for building conduit pipe at that time, corrugated metal pipe, was later found to rust, flatten and leak. Reinforced concrete pipe became the state of the art, and when Duke Power decided to extend the pipe, that is what they used.

- Coal ash is considered an "exempt waste" under the Resource Conservation and Recovery Act, provided it is contained in a pond. Therefore, the Environmental Protection Agency has limited authority. It can only act after a spill.
- Before 2010, power plants in North Carolina were regulated only by the North Carolina Utilities Commission, which was expert on setting rates, but not on engineering and knowledge related to inspecting ash ponds.
- After a change in state law put the North Carolina Department of Energy and Natural Resources (DENR) in charge of regulating the power plants, the agency neglected to pass inspection reports and recommendations to any of the regional offices.
- One of the drainpipes was a matter of concern as early as 1986, when a report said that it was made of corrugated metal (the state of the art material at the time the pipe was installed) throughout most of its length. A map submitted with the next inspection, though, erroneously showed the pipe as reinforced concrete its entire length. Duke officials considered regular inspection for turbidity at the outflow to provide adequate warning of any trouble. The company therefore rejected the recommendation to inspect and compare the water at both ends of the pipe. Video inspection likewise seemed an unnecessary bother.
- In the wake of the Kingston spill, an EPA inspector noticed the pipe and recommended inspections. One of his superiors decided not to mention that recommendation in the final report. He assumed that Duke's practices followed standard industry procedure, ignorant of the pipe's uniqueness and that therefore there could be no standards to follow.
- Without directives or information from either the state or the EPA, regional inspectors had no authority to question the pipe.
- Did any of Duke employees on site have any suspicions about the pipe? If so, did they voice their concerns to superiors? So far as I know, the press has not even asked that question.
- Once employees at the plant noticed the rupture, some engineers, company executives, and government officials went to work quickly and efficiently. Others, unfortunately, did not recognize and communicate the situation's urgency, resulting in bungling that made the problem worse than it needed to be.

Corporate culture affects not only how seriously a company takes environmental matters, but how it responds to the concerns of its employees. The November 2 issue of *Time* reported that jetliners routinely jettisoned about three gallons of kerosene left over from the previous flight every time they took off. The airlines insisted it vaporized and did not return to earth. An Eastern Airlines pilot reported that it contributed to airport smog and fell on runways making them a "greasy and slippery" hazard. When he insisted that mechanics drain the holding tanks on the ground, the airline fired him.

Nowadays many corporations recognize the importance of sustainable practices to their bottom line. Employees who care about environmental matters and report up the chain of command give those corporations a competitive advantage. Far from punishing people for pushing them to be more sustainable, they provide tools and training to empower employees to notice how the company can improve its efforts. Perhaps such a practice in both industry and regulatory agencies will one day interrupt the chain of irresponsible decision-making that has brought about so many manmade natural disasters.

Waste management

But one leading cause of pollution, litter, has nothing to do with industry. Later in the 1970s, when I was in graduate school in Iowa, I participated in a petition drive to get the state legislature to pass a bottle bill. That seemed a great way to cut down on roadside litter. It did not work. The most immediately obvious result of the bottle bill was that vending machines no longer offered drinks in glass bottles. They all switched to aluminum cans, which actually added to the littering problem.

The bottling companies all washed and refilled empty glass bottles. When we bought them at the grocery store, we had to pay a deposit. We got it back when we returned the empties. When we got something from a vending machine, we drank it and then returned it to a nearby bottle rack. The litterbugs who threw glass bottles out their car windows were throwing out money. Other people had incentive to pick up the bottles and redeem them for cash. When all the vending machines switched to aluminum cans nobody collected and recycled the cans. Municipal recycling programs did not exist yet. Meanwhile, the litterbugs kept littering. They just tossed cans that no one had any incentive to pick up. My political activism had not resulted in a solution to the problem. It merely contributed to making another one. A law cannot force people to take personal responsibility. The bottle bill did not even give people an opportunity to exercise personal responsibility.

Litter was and remains only a part of the trash problem. Americans had begun to abandon the habit of separating garbage and trash in the early 1960s. If anyone in the environmental movement seriously advocated returning to it, I do not remember reading about it, and certainly no one paid attention to it. I include waste management as a problem from 1970 that has not been solved. I will later describe consumerism as a problem that has not even been seriously addressed.

Advancing computer technology has given us products unimagined in 1970. Electronic games, and the hardware required to play them, first appeared in 1971, and portable music players in 1979, although not yet computer technology. In the mid 1970s one of my roommates had a fascination with computers that seemed comical. I could hardly mention anything that he would not remind me of a computer application for it. Of course, the phrase "there's an app for that" did not yet exist. Neither did personal desktop computers, but he was building his own and predicted that soon everyone would own one. As I say, I thought he was so wrong it was funny. Within four years, I was renting computer time to finish my doctoral dissertation and wished I had money to buy one. Computers then as now require a printer. The variety and sophistication of peripherals has greatly increased. In addition, we have laptop computers, tablet computers, and smart phones. All of these electronic marvels become obsolete all too soon. Then they become hazardous waste.

Municipalities had basically two waste disposal options in 1970: dumps (renamed landfills) and incinerators. Incinerators have since fallen out of favor for their contribution to air pollution. Because of the popularity of commingling wet garbage and dry trash in the same collection system, landfills became a kind of chemistry experiment that chemistry teachers would never allow students to perform. Let's see what happens if we mix acidic and alkaline wastes together: batteries, old paint, household cleaning supplies that contained ammonia, lye, chlorine bleach, all manner of heavy metals, and so on, and let rainwater percolate through them! The combination leached into the soil and contaminated groundwater, including wells for drinking water.

So little by little, regulations mandated liners for landfills and leachate collectors. Along the way, biological degradation of organic materials slowed to the point that food waste from a decade ago would appear in much the same condition as when it was dumped in the landfill if anyone chose to dig it up. But decomposition has not completely halted. Methane gas (for all practical purposes, brand new natural gas) still accumulates in landfills. Instead of collecting it and using it for energy, landfill operators burn it, which is at least more environmentally friendly than simply letting it escape into the atmosphere.

At least we have come to recognize and identify household hazardous wastes. It is illegal to put toxic or hazardous substances with regular trash. When I moved away from the Chicago area in 2002, the nearby College of DuPage held a one-day collection of old paint, toxic cleaning supplies, and other hazards. The entire concept of hazardous household wastes was fairly novel. To the best of my recollection it was not yet a category of materials that could not be legally put out to the curb with everything else. Now, every county probably has at least one hazardous waste drop-off site.

As landfills reach capacity, it has become more and more difficult to find a place to build a replacement. Not every piece of open land is geologically suitable for building a landfill, and no one has yet built a liner that does not leak. The very thought of a new landfill brings protestors trying to prevent it. Even people who want new landfills do not want them nearby.

What about recycling? In 1970 recycling drop-off centers were few and far between. Not many people used them, anyway. They were too inconvenient. Curbside collection did not exist. When it first started, municipalities asked residents to separate metal, plastic and paper. Recycling rates rose somewhat. Curbside collection was more convenient than drop-off centers, but not convenient enough to encourage large-scale participation. Now most jurisdictions have adopted a single stream recycling system. That reduces the overall market value of the material collected. For example, valuable clean office paper becomes useless for making high-quality recycled paper if it is contaminated by food waste dislodged from an adjacent bottle or can. Recycling rates are still abysmally low—only 34% of material discarded in 2009 entered the recycling stream. Americans recycled just under 60% of aluminum beverage cans, more than double the rate of any other beverage container. When recycling programs started, they were severely limited in the variety of materials they would accept. Fortunately, those Americans who participate in recycling at all can put much more in the recycling can, which means less trash for the landfill.

The August 26 issue of *Time* advocated combating traffic congestion by setting aside pedestrian malls where no vehicular traffic would be allowed. That seemed like a great idea. Many cities tried it and constructed pedestrian malls that lasted for decades. Unfortunately the whole concept turned out to be a dismal failure. People did not patronize the stores in those malls in sufficient numbers to make them economically viable.

Some economists suggested in 1970 that the cost of preventing pollution should be added to the real price of products, and that the economy could adjust. Consumers would therefore have to pay higher costs for manufactured goods, food, energy, and transportation but would have ultimately benefitted from the incentive industry would have to clean up its act. They would also save in doctor bills by not contracting illnesses caused by pollution, for example. It is a plausible hypothesis, but it remains untested. Because industry does not have to bear the cost of preventing pollution, that cost is still passed on to the general public in the form of dealing with it after the fact.

Problems hardly addressed at all.

Hedgpeth noted sarcastically, "It should be obvious even to a Congressman that we should never have learned to make some chemicals in the first place and that certainly we should not be releasing them into the environment . . ." (Hedgpeth 1970). Forty-five years later, it does not seem obvious to anyone in positions of leadership either in government, industry, or the scientific community that there might be scientific or technological questions better left unexplored. Throughout human history (and before) people have eventually exploited new technologies that immediately benefited human society (such as even the most primitive hunters' tools) for destructive purposes (such as those same tools as weapons of war). Hedgpeth was surely neither the first nor the last to hope for some kind of limit to technological and scientific curiosity. But since it is hardwired into the essence of humanity, it should also be obvious, even to the most rabidly anti-technological progressives, that such a limit can occur only by coercion. As much as a few progressives may desire coercion, the vast majority of Americans would regard the cure as worse than the disease.

Commoner proclaimed that the very success of modern technology lay at the root of the environmental crisis that he saw. To many people, the obvious solution would be to design technology that works with nature instead of against it, to approach designing new technology with complete understanding of the various ecological principals it would become a part of. Unfortunately, making hasty decisions to solve an immediate problem may be as much an inherent part of human nature as the urge to explore scientific and technological questions as far as they will lead. I have already described how decisions made to protect the environment by Duke Energy's Dan River Steam Plant eventually caused a coal ash spill.

Benjamin Franklin suggested burning coal instead of wood to preserve forests. On an industrial scale, burning coal and other fossil fuels has caused more environmental problems than it solved. All of the air pollution problems that concerned the environmental movement in 1970 came about as a direct result of burning fossil fuels. Peterson prepared two speculative projections of atmospheric conditions and global temperature by 2020. His optimistic projection depended on the rapid replacement of fossil fuels by nuclear technology (Peterson 1970). In the same issue of the same journal Hedgpeth complained of how the casual treatment of nuclear wastes was already harming the oceans. Forty-five years later, we still have no idea how to handle nuclear wastes. Problems at Chernobyl, Three-Mile Island and Fukushima have greatly diminished the popularity of nuclear energy as an alternative to fossil fuels. But Fukushima illustrates more than the haste to solve one environmental problem with technology that will cause a different one. Engineers designed the reactor very carefully to withstand earthquakes, but no one considered that earthquakes trigger tsunamis and that the facility would be built very close to shore. The world will never know how well the reactor design would have worked in an earthquake, because no one designed any part of the site to withstand the tsunami that destroyed it.

Consumerism

Where Commoner saw technology at the root of environmental degradation, Packard and other social critics saw consumerism. Student groups pointed out that the United States, with 6% of the world's population, consumed half its goods and services. The waste inherent in the production and consumption of this excess directly caused much of the pollution. But as Henry Ford II wrote, "More goods do not necessarily mean more happiness. More goods may eventually mean more junk, and the junk, in the air, in the water, and on the land could make the earth unfit for human habitation before we reach the 21st century" (Shepherd 1970).

The obvious solution is for Americans to consume less. Why is it not happening? The first chapter of this book explored how the entire American economy depends on wasteful production and consumption. Advertisers urge us to spend more and more, regardless of whether their products serve any useful purpose or are the best solution to our needs. Economists and government leaders likewise repeatedly lay the blame for economic troubles on consumers who do not spend enough. The students of the 1970s were the baby boom. Students traditionally have little money of their own. It is easy to recommend that other people spend less, but the recommendation faced two problems. White people made the recommendation, and black people felt that it was just another way of holding them back. And then all the students grew up to start their own careers and families.

If they grew up living in houses built in the 1950s, the average home had only 983 square feet of usable space. The average size of finished space in single-family homes in the 1970s had grown to 1,634 square feet, which was still less than the average size of new houses in the prosperous 1920s. Did the size of houses begin to level off? Not until the housing crisis that began in 2007. By that time, average single-family house size exceeded 2,200 feet. After dropping slightly for about two years, the average size of a home started to increase again, and it now tops 2,400 square feet. Meanwhile, the size of the average household had already decreased between 1950 and 1970 and has continued to decrease. Larger houses occupy still larger lots with fewer people living in them. Within living memory, reel mowers could adequately care for the average yard. As yards grew, power mowers proliferated. At first, it was still necessary to push the mower across the lawn. More and more homeowners now require riding mowers just to tend to grass in reasonable time.

Stuff multiplies to take up available space. I cannot break out the students who advocated consuming less from the generation as a whole. I am not accusing any of them of hypocrisy, but certainly consumerism remains unabated. People still decide what to buy based more on what is in fashion than on what they really need. People still buy and discard single-use products. People still go after fads as silly as pet rocks. Does anyone remember plastic singing fish? Does anyone still have one? If so, does anyone still push the button to make it sing? I suspect that the majority of the fish have made their way to a landfill. With fewer and fewer people living in bigger and bigger houses, some people have accumulated so much stuff that they have more than their house can hold. So they rent storage space for the overflow, and likely as not have only a hazy notion of what they have put there. People still value personal convenience above adopting eco-friendly lifestyles.

Rhetorical irresponsibility

The rhetorical excess of environmentalists in 1970 continues to this day. The scientific literature, which most people did not read, carefully compiled data and took complexities into account when the authors made projections about such issues as the future effects of greenhouse gases and particulate matter on the rise or fall of average global temperatures. Mass media contained the hysterical writings of students, academics writing outside their specialties, and others who cherry picked statistics to warn about the coming ice age, overpopulation, and mass starvation. They wrote with a passion intended to spur industry and government to action motivated by fear and guilt. Just as responsible scientific literature did not become well known to the general public, it remains generally unread today.

Today, environmental spokesmen display their hazy understanding of the nuances of real science to motivate people to make decisions based on fear of global warming. Make no mistake. The earth is warming. Ships can now pass through the Northwest Passage that was permanently iced in when Henry Hudson tried to find it four hundred years ago. Glaciers are melting rapidly. The climate is changing. The trend is real, but the vaunted scientific consensus on the warnings of Al Gore and others is not what they claim.

Several years ago on a visit to my parents, my father and one of my sisters had some fascinating dinner conversation. He was a giant in the field of organizational and industrial psychology. I cannot remember if the conversation took place before or after my sister finished her doctorate in gerontology. His response to something she said was, "Is that real science, or just what gets reported in the *New England Journal of Medicine?*" That surprised me, and I asked for an explanation.

The *New England Journal of Medicine* is one of a number of important journals that publishes only seminal research. That is, studies no one has done before, studies that often make the news the next day. Science reporters who know what they are doing will emphasize that more study is necessary. One study in isolation means little. There is a time-honored process by which seminal research becomes real science. Other teams of scientists must perform the same experiments and obtain the same results. Other scientists must analyze the research procedures and the assumptions and hypotheses behind the study. If the study turns out to be poorly designed it will never become real science. This entire process of testing and judging the study takes place in meetings and is published in journals that never get reported in mass media news reports. Meanwhile, we hear about new study after new study. Or more relevant for the current discussion, we hear repeated claims of impending catastrophe from climate change.

The narrative that human activity alone causes global warming and the only way to combat it is a gigantic international effort to reduce greenhouse gases is not scientific. Nevertheless, we continually hear in the mass media and on social media that climate scientists all agree about climate change. They all agree, we are told, not only that burning fossil fuels and other human activities are causing the glaciers to melt, but that catastrophe lurks just around the corner unless we take drastic action. The people who write and speak on the issue are making exactly the same mistake as those who earlier wrote and spoke about the coming ice age. They are driven by fear and frantically trying to use that fear to motivate everyone else. Fear is not a good way to motivate the general public to agree with a particular viewpoint or take a particular action.

So what does it mean if someone disagrees with that narrative? Progressives insist that they must be dangerously wrong and opposed to scientific knowledge. Unfortunately some scientific organizations themselves have crossed the line between science and propaganda. The American Physical Society has a policy statement that "The evidence is incontrovertible: Global warming is occurring. If no mitigating actions are taken, significant disruptions in the Earth's physical and ecological systems, social systems, security and human health are likely to occur. We must reduce emissions of greenhouse gases beginning now."

Incontrovertible? By definition no scientific statement can be incontrovertible. If any hypothesis warrants credence, it must be falsifiable. That is, if tested with scientific rigor, it must be possible to prove it false. The entire advance of science is based on discovering new information that to some extent falsifies previously accepted hypotheses. Einstein's work falsified some of Newton's. Later scientific study has falsified some of Einstein's. Neither work of falsification could have taken place if the scientific community had deemed the earlier hypotheses incontrovertible.

In September 2011, Ivar Giaever, a Nobel-Prize winning physicist, resigned from the American Physical Society because of that statement. In January 2012, 16 distinguished scientists wrote in the *Wall Street Journal* that a growing number of scientists disagree with the need for drastic action on global warming. Are they dangerously wrong and opposed to scientific knowledge? Notice: they did not disagree about the reality of global warming, but only with a particular political narrative about what to do about it. Are they a tiny minority, out of step with the majority of their colleagues? Anyone who makes such a charge has no factual information to back it up. As the article points out, not all scientists who agree with the authors' policy position are willing to sign their names.

Although the number of publicly dissenting scientists is growing, many young scientists furtively say that while they also have serious doubts about the global-warming message, they are afraid to speak up for fear of not being promoted—or worse. They have good reason to worry. In 2003, Dr. Chris de Freitas, the editor of the journal Climate Research, dared to publish a peer-reviewed article with the politically incorrect (but factually correct) conclusion that the recent warming is not unusual in the context of climate changes over the past thousand years. The international warming establishment quickly mounted a determined campaign to have Dr. de Freitas removed from his editorial job and fired from his university position. Fortunately, Dr. de Freitas was able to keep his university job.

This is not the way science is supposed to work, but we have seen it before—for example, in the frightening period when Trofim Lysenko hijacked biology in the Soviet Union. Soviet biologists who revealed that they believed in genes, which Lysenko maintained were a bourgeois fiction, were fired from their jobs. Many were sent to the gulag and some were condemned to death. (Allegre et al., 2012)

Since the global warming establishment has declared the need for mitigating actions "incontrovertible," they saw fit to punish the editor of a professional journal for publishing a peer-reviewed article that they did not like. If Dr. de Freitas had tenure in 2003, the attempt to get him fired was not only vindictive but illegal. Academic tenure exists solely for the purpose of shielding scholars from dismissal because of their professional viewpoints, no matter how out of touch they may be with the majority of their colleagues. Punishing heretics is not the business of science. It has historically been an abuse of power in religion. Now it happens all the time in politics. Can anyone say RINOs? Meanwhile, projections of global warming issued by the Intergovernmental Panel on Climate Change (IPCC) appear to be based on a particular computer model that has consistently failed to predict what real measurements show.

Speaking at the World Climate Summit that took place in Cancun, Mexico in December 2010, Ted Turner expressed his frustration at the movement's failure to motivate the masses. "When," he asked, "will the world understand that we are right and they are wrong?" (Bennett and Williams, 2011). The sheer arrogance of that statement, especially coming from someone with no scientific credentials whatsoever, is breathtaking. *An Inconvenient Truth* appeared only in 2006, and Al Gore, whose scientific credentials equal Turner's, traveled the world to lecture on the subject. And a whole four years later, not everyone in the world fell into line with its conclusions. Scolding is not a good way to motivate the general public to agree with a particular viewpoint or take a particular action.

In 2009, Colin Beavan published a book titled *No Impact Man: The Adventures of a Guilty Liberal Who Attempts to Save the Planet, and the Discoveries He Makes About Himself and Our Way of Life in the Process.* I noted earlier that fear motivates writers and speakers about the coming global warming catastrophe. From Beavan's subtitle it is apparent that guilt does, too. Guilt is not a good way to motivate the general public to agree with a particular viewpoint or take a particular action. Fear, scolding, and guilt are especially ineffective if the desired viewpoint follows the well-worn path of earlier failed predictions.

Polls indicate that about 16% of the American public believes both that the earth is warming and that drastic effort is required to avert catastrophe. The issue motivates them to make drastic sacrifices in their own lifestyles as well as scold the rest of the public. About 18% of the public view environmental issues with hostility or indifference. That leaves 66% of the public that claim to value an environmentally friendly lifestyle, although there is a noticeable gap between what they say they value and how they confess that they live. These people may or may not believe that the climate is warming. Some of them may even agree that only some kind of drastic action will prevent catastrophe.

Their expressed beliefs do not control their actions, in part because they find the attitude of the 16% offensive. There is a common stereotype of the "greenie" (a young woman with money who votes Democratic and looks like a hippie) who looks down her nose at anyone who doesn't drive a Prius and is not vegan, or at least vegetarian. She works for environmental street credibility by campaigning for political candidates who will vote for expensive and intrusive government programs.

I have often expressed the view that climate change rhetoric generates more heat than light and does not help the development and acceptance of sustainability. When I made that point to a Linked-In group, I received some very enlightening responses. Here is one important paragraph:

> However, if you cannot get action on the problem of Global Warming, with its capacity to destroy most of life on earth, it seems unlikely to me that less catastrophic problems are likely to override the profit motive and get real action.

Override the profit motive! I gather the person who wrote that is an academic. As a lifelong academic myself, I understand the style. Unless they teach in a college of business, academics aren't professionally concerned with economics, the structure and role of business, or anything else connected with the idea of profit. Politically, many faculty, staff, and students at our colleges and universities view the whole concept of profit with suspicion. Colleges and universities are non-profit institutions.

People in an academic community who are not professionally concerned with aspects of business may or may not be interested in learning about it. Most academics I know have broad interests and know a great deal about other subjects besides what they teach. I suspect that the people with the strongest political suspicions of profit have the least actual knowledge and understanding of it. I might have easily joined that number if I had not worked in a bookstore during my entire time as an undergraduate and learned first hand something about how a business operates.

What actions are truly necessary to prevent climate change from causing a catastrophe? Short of massive international bureaucracies to ban industrial activity, they are all necessary for some other reason. For example, why should we control greenhouse gas emissions? Doing so will enhance air quality and therefore public health. Let's stop arguing over whether coal-fired power plants are making glaciers melt and find a way to make them obsolete.

Fringe elements in the 1970s chose to express themselves with symbolic and confrontational actions, many of which were antisocial and some of which were criminal. It is bad enough for the reputation of the environmental movement that some who have made drastic personal lifestyle changes appear to disapprove of anyone who has not. Confrontational behaviors, such as the recent occupy movement, likewise repel more people than they attract. The chairman of President Nixon's Council on Environmental Controls Russell Train warned the activists of his day, "We can't govern by protest, demonstration, and litigation." It is past time for today's activists to take that warning to heart.

In 1970, environmental issues united the country, but from all the teach-in leaders said and wrote, it appeared that only the government and big business had any particular responsibility. The general public was allowed to think that environmental responsibility was something for "them" to do and not "us." Now that the role of the individual is more clearly recognized, but the issues no longer unite the country, too much of the public views environmental advocates as "them" and not "us."

A new problem since 1970: Political polarization

Earth Day succeeded beyond all expectations. Hardly anyone publicly admitted to being opposed to the environmental movement for more than a decade afterward. But Americans have a short attention span, and eventually the environment ceased to be an important issue in elections, having been supplanted by terrorism, war, health care, abortion, LGBT issues, and more.

Conservation efforts are no longer regarded either as a communist plot or a smokescreen to distract the public from more important issues. Nowadays, however, opposition to environmental protection no longer comes from both sides of the political spectrum. The main opposition comes either from industries that find it a threat or people who have hijacked the label "conservative" and fail to recognize that "conservation" comes from the same root.

Environmental activists bear much of the blame. Their gloom and doom prophecies do not play as well as they did 45 years ago. The more vocal environmentalists find it offensive that most of the public does not share their alarm over climate change. So they scold and try to force the public to believe that they are right and everyone else is wrong. When will they catch on that no one is listening and advocate for the environment with issues most of the public already cares about? Surely the real issue ought to be how to persuade people to adopt more sustainable habits for whatever reason appeals to them, not make the whole public agree with a particular viewpoint.

Much of industry has returned to its pre-Earth Day stance that environmental regulations pose an unreasonable burden. It found an early champion in Tom DeLay. After graduating from the University of Houston in 1970, DeLay became a chemist for a pesticide manufacturer. He purchased his own pest control business in 1973, and in that capacity began his life-long war against the EPA and the way it regulated his industry. He fought not only with that agency, but the IRS, the government of Texas when it decided to require licensure for exterminators, and basically any government entity that stood in the way of his doing exactly what he wanted to do. He was particularly angry when the EPA outlawed Mirex, practically the only tool useful tool against fire ants. By that time, he had become the first Republican elected from his state house district since Reconstruction. At some time (no site where I have found the quotations provides dates) he called the Environmental Protection Agency "the Gestapo of government" and "a bunch of jack-booted thugs." He called the Nobel committee for chemistry "Swedish environmental extremists." He was elected to Congress in 1984.

When Ronald Reagan ran for President in 1980 after half a century of steady growth of both the numbers and power of federal regulatory agencies, some kind of push for deregulation was inevitable. Since the Republican Party had long been the more sensitive of the two major political parties to industrial interests,

Republican leadership in deregulation was likewise inevitable. There seems to be no reason, however, for national Republicans as a whole to have become enemies of the environmental movement, which had always enjoyed bipartisan support. Republicans supported conservation and other environmental issues from the time President Grant established Yellowstone as the first national park through the landmark environmental legislation of the Nixon administration. Although Reagan ordered removal of the solar panels President Carter had installed in the White House, he was no enemy of environmental causes. The Reagan administration approved ten of the environmental laws listed at the beginning of this chapter. Five more followed during George H. W. Bush's single term in office. Two came from the Clinton administration's two terms.

The list of environmental legislation at the beginning of this chapter ends in 1999 not because the sources are old and obsolete, but because the collapse of bipartisanship in the federal government has not allowed any more laws to be passed in this century. Nearly every major federal environmental law was enacted by cooperation between a Republican President and Democrats who controlled both houses of Congress. The Republican Party, under the leadership of Newt Gingrich, gained control of the House of Representatives in 1994 for the first time since the Truman administration. Delay, by the way, became majority whip. Gingrich was an effective minority leader because of his attack-dog style. He did not succeed in changing his style to something more suitable for serving as Speaker of the House and leading a majority. Speaker Dennis Hastert declined to bring legislation to a vote unless a majority of the majority favored it, which made bipartisan cooperation difficult. Nancy Pelosi as Democratic speaker continued Hastert's divisive leadership style. Senate leaders in both parties took no steps to enhance bipartisan cooperation.

President Bush proved no more adaptable to new political realties, a Congress controlled by Democrats in his last two years in office, than Gingrich had. President Obama slammed the door on bipartisanship with his tactics for pushing his health care initiative through Congress. A constant stream of Democrats visited the White House so that the President could persuade any of them with other views of how the law should be written to accept his way. He did not meet or speak with Republicans. The law passed without any input from or even consultation with the Republican minority. Pelosi famously said, "We have to pass the bill so you can find out what is in it—away from the fog of the controversy."

But what was the fog of the controversy? Republicans who had been kept completely in the dark nevertheless issued stern warnings and criticisms, some of which were probably wide of the mark, based on their incomplete knowledge. Obama and Pelosi preferred to ignore and dismiss Republican concerns rather than discuss the contents of the law transparently and openly or seek input from any of the Republicans whom Obama later acknowledged had shown leadership on the issue. Since the Republicans retook control of the House of Representatives in 2010, neither the President nor congressional leaders of either party have shown the slightest willingness to compromise on anything. There is no center left in American politics. Both parties have become beholden to their extremists in the selection of candidates for federal offices.

Chapter 4 – What now, and who is responsible?

The collapse of bipartisanship in politics and the division between "us" and "them" in public discourse makes the way forward very difficult. Yet every April 22 is still Earth Day. In 1970 the teach-in and related demonstrations got most of the press. They may have also constituted the most important actions. Since then, the strength of Earth Day has always been grassroots involvement in doing something about local issues. Every year, people gather together to collect trash, uproot non-native invasive weeds, plant trees, and other physical acts to improve the environment of their own communities.

There is nothing like participating with other people in a project to sensitize us to our own habits. One year when I was helping to pull up ivy, honeysuckle, and other unwanted vines from an area that was to be transformed into a habitat for native plants, another participant held up a long ivy vine and declared that she would never buy any of it even in pots. As far as I am concerned, ivy is not a weed if it is growing where you want it, but I chose other ground covers for my property long before that day. I am glad I learned how to identify honeysuckle. That is what, if unchecked, will choke out what I planted. Now that I know what it is and what it does, I can pull it.

The experience of cleaning trash out of a stream similarly causes people to promise themselves that they will never again throw trash out of a car or just dump it wherever they happen to be when they finish with something, or at least it ought to.

A new concept: sustainability

By the late 1960s, conservationists had begun to call themselves environmentalists instead. They had expanded the scope of their interests and activities, and the older term no longer adequately described them. The scope of the environmental movement, which now often goes by the name of "green," has continued to expand. Here are just some new concerns in recent decades:

- Recognition of the environmental impact of individual choices
- Reduction of the carbon footprint (itself a new concept) of both individuals and industry

- Concern for the worldwide effects of deforestation and otherwise clearing of open space.
- Development of renewable energy sources
- Reduction in the size of the waste stream
- Reduction of the toxicity of the waste stream and runoff
- Development and encouragement of green building practices to reduce the environmental impact of new and remodeled buildings
- Greater recognition of the environmental impact of food
- Recognition of dangers from lawn-treatment chemicals
- Recognition of dangers from household cleaning products
- Concern for the effect of chemicals in cosmetics, shampoo, and other personal care products
- Concern for the effect of chemicals used for food packaging and food storage
- Concern for the proliferation of disposable plastic
- Discovery of a huge patch of plastic debris and other trash in the oceans
- Concern for the rising cost of natural resources and maintaining our wasteful ways
- Recognition that America is not the only economic powerhouse, as it was right after the Second World War and that "emerging nations" want the same amenities we enjoy, and therefore compete with us for natural resources, and therefore
- Concern for the health and livelihood of foreign workers who have begun to make such a large portion of consumer goods
- Fair trade practices for importation of raw materials, produce, crafts, etc.

Although no one has stopped using the term "environmentalism," more and more environmental leaders have come to recognize that "sustainability" better represents the scope of these new concerns. Sustainability is often described as having three pillars: environmental, economic, and social. None can stand without both of the others.

- Everyone's living conditions are **viable** with a combination of environmental and economic sustainability—at least until social unrest overwhelms it.
- Everyone's living conditions are **bearable** with a combination of environmental and social sustainability—at least until they all run out of money to keep it going.

⁓ Everyone's living conditions are **equitable** with a combination of social and economic sustainability—at least until the environment degrades to a point that the earth can no longer sustain life.

⁓ Everyone's living conditions are **sustainable** only where the three basic kinds of sustainability intersect.

It is easy enough to find definitions of the principles and goals of sustainability. It is less easy to envision what actions either promote or hinder achievement of sustainability. The International Brundtland Commission Report of 1987 issued a widely quoted definition: "Sustainable development is development that meets the needs of the present without compromising the ability of future generations to meet their own needs." To put is more simply, it means practices we can continue indefinitely without causing harm to the environment, the economy, or to people. But how can we determine what practices are indeed sustainable? An international initiative called The Natural Step helps describe a sustainable society in a way that we can actually form a practical mental image using two metaphors.

First, the current model of development resembles a **funnel**. Right now, worldwide, the demand for and consumption of resources has outgrown nature's ability to replenish. As demand increases, capacity to meet it declines. Over time, societies move to the narrower part of the funnel, where there are fewer options. We need to open the funnel. Second, we are beginning to recognize that we must examine whole systems, how everything works together. Consider a **tree**. For any large system, the trunk and branches of a tree represent the core framework, the basic operating principles of the system. The leaves represent the details. To reword a familiar cliché, we cannot afford to be like someone who cannot see the tree because of all the leaves. If the funnel represents how we damage nature by systematically increasing demands on it, the tree trunk represents areas where we must stop this systematic increase.

The Natural Step has worked out four principles it considers both necessary and enough to achieve sustainability: extraction of substances, concentration of substances, physical degradation of nature, and basic human needs. They apply to any scale of any activity, and they do not overlap. The repeated use of the phrase "systematic increase" explicitly means that the principles do not include prohibitions of any of the actions described. A sustainable society can still cut down trees, mine for metals, eat fish, and so on. It just must not keep doing so past nature's ability to replenish.

1. To become a sustainable society we must eliminate our contributions to the *systematic increase* of concentrations of substances extracted from the Earth's crust (for example, heavy metals and fossil fuels).

The Earth's crust is the outer layer that we live on. We share it with other animals and plants. We have cut down trees, eaten and clothed ourselves with animals and animal products, and depended on the soil to grow crops for millennia.

Humans have extracted resources from beneath the surface from the first time anyone recognized the usefulness of metals. In addition to ancient metals like iron, copper, gold, and silver, we have in recent centuries identified and found uses for mercury, zinc, platinum, aluminum, and many others. The Earth's crust provides its substances in limited amounts. We have already used up all of the petroleum and natural gas in North America that was easily accessible. And so we must engage in more expensive processes and more hazardous activities like deep sea drilling and hydraulic fracturing in order to extract any more. True to form, these activities move forward in the complete absence of any scientific assurance that they will not cause an environmental disaster some time in the future.

2. To become a sustainable society we must eliminate our contributions to the *systematic increase* of concentrations of substances produced by society (for example, plastics, dioxins, PCBs and DDT).

If you have ever read about ancient practices for tanning leather or making metal alloys, you know that humanity has a long history of making and using noxious substances in unsafe working conditions. Today, we have greater concern for workplace safety, but the number and scale of manmade substances has greatly increased over the past century, or even the past few decades. Unlike manmade substances of the past, the ones The Natural Step explicitly mentions do not naturally break down and become something else. Plastic breaks down into smaller and smaller pieces, but remains plastic. We do not yet know all of the ecological consequences of all the little bits of plastic in soil, rivers, or oceans. What we do know is troublesome.

Dioxins, a family of toxic and often carcinogenic chemicals, basically have no use whatsoever. PCBs (polychlorinated biphenyls) used to be manufactured in large quantities until banned in 1977. Otherwise no one manufactures dioxins. They are unintended byproducts of combustion that first pollute the air and then settle on land and in water. From there they enter the food supply and bioaccumulate. That is, organisms low on the food chain ingest them and do not excrete them. They enter the bodies of organisms higher on the food chain and never go away. Levels of dioxins in the environment have declined since the banning of PCBs, but not enough for exposure levels to cease to remain a concern. Most people have detectable levels of dioxins and other undesirable chemicals in their bodies.

3. To become a sustainable society we must eliminate our contributions to the *systematic* physical degradation of nature and natural processes (for example, over harvesting forests, destroying habitat and overfishing).

Cape Cod in Massachusetts was named for a fish that seemed to be in infinite supply. Not any more. Cod is but one kind of fish subject to severe restrictions on fishing and not the most seriously overfished. Much of the world used to be covered with trees. Too often, in recent years, people have clear-cut trees all over the world in order to put the land to other uses. Adverse environmental consequences of deforestation are too numerous even to begin to describe in this chapter. Trees and fish are renewable resources, but not if they are harvested or destroyed at a rate beyond their capacity to reproduce. How can any society thrive after the last tree has been cut down and the last edible fish eaten?

4. To become a sustainable society we must eliminate our contributions to conditions that *systematically* undermine people's capacity to meet their basic human needs (for example, unsafe working conditions and not enough pay to live on).

The first three principles describe environmental sustainability. They do not necessarily express any of the new concerns that have arisen since the 1970s, although they certainly encompass them. This fourth principle describes the more recent recognition of social sustainability. The Natural Step's principles do not directly address economic sustainability.

According to The Natural Step's description, social sustainability does not require the absence of unemployment, hunger, or violence. It does not require the elimination of all social inequality. These problems are hardwired into human nature. All human society at any time or any place on earth has included some kind of evil exploitation of the weak by the strong. But today, we can no longer think of any one society as unrelated to all or most others on the planet. Social sustainability means that regardless of social class or nationality, no one in the world finds it impossible to meet basic human needs.

Not everything that seems "green" is sustainable. For example, sustainability requires that we stop burning fossil fuels, or as President George W. Bush put it, get over our addiction to oil. We have discovered that in addition to polluting the environment, our consumption of oil, both as a fuel and as a raw material in manufacturing, contributes to an unstable geopolitical climate, in which we must import oil from nations that share few if any or our national values.

In the 1970s, many thoughtful environmentalists looked to nuclear energy as the logical replacement for fossil fuels, at least when it came to generation of electricity. Yet at the same time, other thoughtful environmentalists noticed that nuclear plants were treating spent fuel rods very carelessly and releasing radiation not only into the air, but into the water. Subsequent nuclear accidents quickly took the luster off nuclear energy. There are still thoughtful environmentalists who prefer nuclear power to burning fossil fuels, but until someone devises a creative and viable solution to the problem of nuclear wastes, it will not be sustainable.

So renewable energy ought to replace fossil fuels. Right? Eventually, yes, but technological, financial, and political barriers remain. At least one kind of solar development appears inherently unsustainable. In December 2011, what was then world's largest solar plant, Andasol, began operating on Spain's Gaudix plateau in Andalusia. It uses 600,000 parabolic mirrors to produce 150 megawatts of electricity, enough to power a city of 500,000. The parabolic mirrors do not operate on the same principles as the more familiar solar panels. Instead of directly creating electrical current, they absorb heat from the sun, which is transferred to some 30,000 tons of salt for storage. That heat operates steam turbines, meaning that Andasol can continue to produce electricity for about eight hours after sunset. The Gaudix plateau is about 3,600 feet above sea level. At that altitude, the air is clearer and less turbulent than at lower altitudes. That is why Gaudix captures more energy from the sun than the Saudi Arabian peninsula. Solar Energy Generating Systems has built a similar but larger project in California's Mohave Desert.

Both will be dwarfed if an international venture called Desertec Industrial Initiative succeeds in its plans to build a Sahara-wide solar plant. The Sahara receives more energy from the sun in six hours than the entire world uses in a year. The project as planned could produce 15% of Europe's electricity by mid-century. Are these massive parabolic mirror projects the future of solar energy? They do not seem sustainable to me. They are at once too big and too small. What if every project that anyone has ever thought of gets built and produces the maximum possible amount of electricity? It will not make enough of a dent in the world's demands for power to justify the environmental costs of building them.

The Andasol project received massive funding from European governments. By the time it was completed, the governments had begun to scale back their support. The world economy tanked and the euro became threatened by massive debt among some eurozone members. Parabolic mirror projects will find it much more difficult than Andasol to raise funding. Besides coming on line in a more favorable economic climate, the Gaudix plateau has important advantages lacking in other sites. Besides receiving 2,000 hours of sunlight annually at a fairly high altitude, it has ample underground springs to provide water for the turbines. Even more important, a high-voltage power line already existed nearby.

In the California desert, it is necessary to build the infrastructure before it is possible to distribute the electricity. America's antiquated power grid cannot get electricity from remote solar or wind farms to where it is needed without major overhaul. Southern California already has to import massive amounts of water from long distances to support its current population and industry. Where will it get more water to boil for steam turbines?

And the Sahara? As envisioned, the project will begin in relatively stable Morocco. If its developers truly intend to build across the entire Sahara, they will need cooperation from much less stable governments–and the local population, which harbors ter-rorists in some locations. Add security concerns to the lack of water and existing infrastructure. Does anyone seriously expect the people of northern Africa to acquiesce to such a massive project for the benefit of providing electricity to Europe? After all, why should they?

The Andasol project now produces clean energy. Because of the electricity it provides, it keeps 500,000 tons of carbon dioxide annually from being pumped into the atmosphere. But what about preparing all of that land for construction? What about manufacturing all of that equipment? Making the equipment for parabolic mirror installations requires massive amounts of steel. Since the solar plants cannot operate until they are built, making the steel and manufacturing the equipment relies on fossil fuels. Meanwhile, it will take years to build any more huge projects. At some point, the design will have to be set in concrete, so to speak, while technological innovation will continue. Could delays in construction of some projects render them obsolete by the time they are ready to go on line? What happens to the land and equipment after the site's designed lifespan ends?

Returning to The Natural Step's metaphor of the tree, we must not focus on the trunk and branches of the tree and neglect the leaves. Probably no one of us can relate to the daunting task of keeping the entire tree of sustainability healthy. But we can envision a cluster of leaves along one small branch. We can look out for the sustainability of our own individual lifestyle and the community in which we live. We can be mindful of people across the world—or across town—that suffer from inequality and injustice. We can remember that everyone is interconnected with everyone else. We can think globally as we act locally.

The top priority for achieving sustainability must be to make it seem normal and ordinary, not a special interest of a self-appointed elite, as it so often seems in our current polarized society. We will have a sustainable world when we all take responsibility for our own part in opening the funnel by greening our lifestyles, when sustainability does not seem like something for some diffuse and indefinable "them" to do, but rather something concrete and visible for "us" to do.

Some things ordinary people can and should do

Be politically active if you want, but it is more important to remember that you have daily influence with your family, the people you see in your neighborhood, the people you work with, and your own work place. Share your knowledge. Talk about your interests and concerns. And live out a sustainable lifestyle where others can see it.

Be careful not to litter, and participate with others in projects such as picking up litter from streets or streams. Parents, make sure your children understand why not to litter. There are many reasons, of course, but here is one: all kinds of litter eventually make it into the ocean. Pictures of birds that starved to death after filling their stomachs with plastic might pack an emotional punch, but people look, shudder, look away and forget. And so a possibly more persuasive reason for taking action on litter is that ocean pollution from littering also interferes with fish and fishing. It directly takes money out of our pockets in the price of seafood.

Be mindful of what you buy. Do you really need it? Is it quality that will last, so you do not have to throw it out after a little while? Can you find the products with the least packaging so that you do not take home excessive trash along with your purchases? Are the products' ingredients good for the environment as you use them? Participate fully in recycling programs, including your hazardous household waste facility. Recycling was impossible in 1970, because it did not occur to anyone with ability to implement it until later. Recycling is actually the third of the three Rs of the environment: reduce, reuse, recycle. To reduce,

- Sort through your trash a few times before taking it to the curb in order to know what you are discarding and what takes the most space. Look for ways to adjust your habits so you will discard less bulk.
- Keep up with routine maintenance so your appliances do not prematurely become a waste disposal problem
- Buy quality. The lowest priced item can be tempting, but good products last longer. Good products can easily outlast two or three of the cheap ones.
- Buy in bulk when possible.
- But do not buy more of anything than you need, especially if it is perishable.
- Do not buy toxic products if there is a feasible non-toxic alternative.
- Prefer to buy reusable items instead of disposables.
- Prefer plug-in products to those that require batteries. Even disposable batteries wear out eventually. Dead batteries ought to be treated as hazardous waste.
- Choose minimal packaging.

⌒ Avoid impulse buying.

⌒ Do not buy anything you will not use regularly if it is possible to rent or borrow it.

⌒ Reduce junk mail and paper bills.

To reuse,

⌒ Donate to and patronize thrift stores.

⌒ Buy remanufactured, refurbished, or rebuilt products.

⌒ As much as possible, repair or restore belongings instead of discarding them.

⌒ If you subscribe to print magazines, let someone else use them when you have finished reading them.

⌒ Use salvaged or recycled materials when building or remodeling your home.

⌒ When you garden, return plastic trays and pots to where you purchased the plants.

To increase your recycling,

⌒ Put recycling containers near every wastebasket to make recycling as convenient as possible.

⌒ Search for ways to recycle what your municipal program does not accept.

⌒ Compost yard waste, food waste, and other organic material.

⌒ If you have no need for compost, find somewhere that accepts material for composting, such as a community garden.

⌒ Think about what to do about the end of a product's useful life before you buy it.

⌒ Consider how to reuse and recycle before remodeling or building a house.

⌒ Reuse or recycle clothing to shabby to donate. The fibers themselves have value.

⌒ If you change the oil in your car yourself, recycle the used oil.

⌒ Buy recycled products.

Keep looking for more ways to save energy and water. If you have not had your dryer vent cleaned in the past two years, doing so can make a big difference (not to mention reducing chances of a house fire). Even little things like fastening your seat belt before you start the car can add up. At work, if you see something that has the potential to do or reduce environmental damage, pass your concerns up the hierarchy. If you speak up, maybe someone will do something about it. If you say nothing, who else will know the potential danger or opportunity? Remember that you are not alone. What would be the environmental impact of several hundred million people living as you live?

If everyone in the country adopted each of these recommendations to the level of drastic lifestyle change, it would still not be enough to achieve sustainability. For example, cleaning up creeks and rivers is good, but citizen effort cannot restore them to their original condition. Streams and rivers bear the scars of many decades of serving as dumping grounds for industrial waste, along with the more recent problem of agricultural runoff. Individuals likewise do not make decisions about large systems like waste management or production and distribution of electricity.

The need for education of the public

Chances are, since you have purchased and read this book, you try to keep informed about environmental matters. Not everyone does. The Associated Press in conjunction with the National Opinion Research Center conducted a poll (Tomson, 2012) to study the public's understanding of and action on issues related to energy. It stands to reason that a poll about other environmental issues would yield comparable results. Polltakers made seven statements and asked whether each one was a major reason, a minor reason, or not a reason at all for America's energy problems. Here are two of them:

- People use a lot of energy and they are not willing to reduce that demand.
- People use a lot of energy and they do not know how to reduce that demand.

It strikes me as odd, to say the least, that while 60% of respondents considered the latter, people's ignorance of how to reduce energy demand, a major reason, even more, 64%, called people's unwillingness a major reason. So most people recognize that the general public is not well informed, but even more of them pointed to people's (meaning other people's?) unwillingness to change as a major problem. Who has a large amount of responsibility for increasing energy savings according to this poll?

- Energy industry, 65%
- Federal government, 58%
- Individuals, 57%
- Businesses, 54%
- State and local government, 50%

Meanwhile, 18% said that the U.S. government has little or no responsibility, 13% that individuals have little to no responsibility. Only 41% believe that the actions of individuals can make much difference at all. Part of educating the public, therefore, entails pointing out the power of crowds. One person using cloth shopping bags instead of accepting plastic makes little difference. Tens of millions of people, or better, hundreds of millions of people using cloth shopping bags makes a huge difference—not only regarding pollution, but the energy required to manufacture all those plastic bags.

Overall, it appears that we know a little bit about all sorts of issues and programs related to energy, but not much in particular about any of them. Most of us get information from TV news or newspapers, but don't trust it much. The poll asked about ten different sources of information. Only information from local utility companies was considered completely or very trustworthy by a majority of the respondents. Its score was only 52%. Three fourths of us know that both governments and utility companies have more programs designed to help people save energy than there were 10 years ago, but not nearly that many people know much in particular about any of them.

For all the political controversy lately about phasing out incandescent light bulbs, it surprises me that only 46% of respondents considered that they knew a lot about the issue. Fewer than 20% reported knowing a lot about LEED certification and four other choices. Those of us engaged in educating the public have our work cut out for us, especially if we publish online. I do not know what it means that only just over 10% said they "completely or very much trust" websites. After all, the best place to find information from local utilities, consumer groups, various levels of government, etc. is their own web sites.

The power of large entities: academia and business

I received my first introduction to the term "sustainability" when the faculty senate at the university where I worked created a sustainability committee and invited people from faculty, students, administration, and facilities staff to join it. The committee was divided into a number of different working groups, and I participated first in "green buildings." Two members of the facilities staff had just earned LEED certification. When a working group for water and energy use was added the following year, I joined that one instead.

LEED (Leadership in Energy and Environmental Design) is one of the projects of the U.S. Green Building Council, "a 501(c)(3) nonprofit organization committed to a prosperous and sustainable future for our nation through cost-efficient and energy-saving green buildings." A variety of different building projects can qualify for LEED certification. These include new construction, major renovations, and upgrading the operation and maintenance of existing buildings. In addition, there are standards specifically for commercial interiors, retail space, schools, healthcare facilities, private residences, and neighborhood development. Achieving certification requires meeting basic prerequisites and then earning points in five major categories:

- Sustainable sites—strategies to minimize impact on ecosystems and water resources
- Water efficiency—strategies to minimize the use of potable water and promote better use of water both inside and outside
- Energy and atmosphere—strategies to promote better energy performance of a building
- Materials and resources—strategies to use sustainable building materials and reduce waste
- Indoor environmental quality—strategies that promote both better indoor air quality and access to daylight

Depending on the number of points earned, a project can receive certification at four different levels: Certified, Silver, Gold, and Platinum.

LEED, as an arm of a non-profit corporation, represents one way that sustainability is moving forward despite the utter dysfunction of the federal government. The university where I worked now requires that all construction and major remodeling of buildings must meet LEED Silver level standards. Regarding energy and water, facilities personnel replaced old electric and water meters, upgraded HVAC systems, installed occupancy detectors to turn lights on and off automatically, found and corrected water leaks, installed low-flow toilets and otherwise systematically undertook projects to use less energy and water, reduce greenhouse gas emissions, and, not so incidentally, save the university millions of dollars. It has devoted similar attention and achieves similar savings in transportation and other activities in which I was not personally involved. The university's sustainable efforts have made great progress since I left the committee. Probably every college and university of any size likewise operates a formal sustainability program.

Large corporations are are building sustainability into their operations. Many have redesigned delivery routes to save fuel or replaced still usable equipment with more energy efficient models. Many manufacturers have reduced packaging for their products and/or committed to using recycled plastic and other materials to make them. Several have worked hard to achieve zero waste to landfill. Some corporate sustainability projects require elaborate planning. On the other hand, changes can be so simple, that once someone thinks of it, they see it should have been obvious much earlier. For instance, Massachusetts Container Corporation, which sells printed corrugated boxes, began to schedule all printings of the same color to be run at once and sequenced the daily schedule to begin with the lightest colors and end with the darkest. Those simple and obvious changes meant that they had to wash their equipment less frequently and therefore saved millions of gallons of water.

Many companies also design and manufacture "green" products. Unfortunately others make unsubstantiated green claims, which has given rise to the term "greenwashing." Perhaps the earliest green products were those manufactured from recycled material. A college I worked for during the 1990s exclusively purchased recycled paper for printers and copiers—grayish, stiff paper that regularly clogged up the machines. Because of low quality, high prices and unsubstantiated environmental claims, "green" products acquired a poor reputation. The quality of recycled paper now cannot be distinguished from virgin paper. The quality of recycled products in general has similarly been improved. Because the recycling process remains unfinished until some manufacturer makes products from post-consumer and post-industrial waste and sells them, the rest of us ought to prefer recycled products whenever they are available. They may be more expensive than regular products, but buy them anyway. The retail price of anything includes the amount of time it stays on store shelves. All else being equal, the product that moves the fastest will have the lowest price. When enough people buy the recycled product instead of the one made from virgin materials, the recycled product will become the less expensive.

A number of companies, some dating back to the first Earth Day itself, started up for the purpose of making and selling products for cleaning and personal care without the use of synthetic chemicals. Burt's Bees, Tom's of Maine, and Seventh Generation became especially successful and well known. They have experienced some of the familiar outcomes of entrepreneurial success. The founders of Burt's Bees and Tom's of Maine sold their companies to larger companies, Clorox and Colgate-Palmolive respectively. The board of Seventh Generation fired its founder and CEO, Jeffrey Hollender, after 23 years. The more mindlessly anti-corporate environmentalists have claimed that the first two sold out to corporate interests, that Burt's Bees is now nothing more than Clorox and Tom's of Maine is nothing more than Colgate-Palmolive.

I find Clorox especially admirable, though. Chlorine bleach, its signature product, is toxic and corrosive. Its vapors not only stink and make people's eyes water, they damage the tissues of the respiratory system. They also contribute to the fact that in many places, indoor air quality is worse than outdoor air. From the makers of DDT onward, many companies who find their products subject to criticism on environmental or health grounds have circled the wagons and vigorously defended themselves. They have ridiculed and attempted to debunk scientific evidence of the harm their products cause. They have gone on the offensive in the courts. They have poured campaign contributions into the coffers of politicians whom they expect to sponsor legislation that protects them and oppose legislation that limits their freedom to continue to operate unchecked. Clorox, on the other hand, started a new division, Green Works, which competes against its traditional lines with products that contain no chlorine bleach.

As for Seventh Generation, the board did not fire Hollender because his vision was too green for the company to make sufficient profit. Among other things, it decided he had failed to make truly sustainable products. And he has admitted as much.

> Seventh Generation was never a sustainable brand, not even close. I struggle to find any truly sustainable brand, though I continue to look. The problem is that we've confused less bad with good. The fact that we make chlorine free paper towels with 100% post consumer waste doesn't make the product good- it's just less bad....

[Climate change is coming faster than we can imagine] All we've been able to do is tap lightly on the breaks of the car that is hurling towards the wall (Boynton, 2011)

The role of science and technology

In 1970 Barry Commoner and others took a dim view of technology. The environmental problems that disturbed them so much seemed like the outcome not of inadequate technologies, but the very most successful ones. Some environmentalists today vocally oppose any advanced technology on principle. Commoner mentioned a method of wastewater treatment, now long obsolete, that accounted for only half of a natural cycle. Its failure to account for the other half contributed greatly to algae blooms. To whatever extent Commoner's pessimism about technology is justified, there is no chance that it will stop. My own reservations about parabolic mirrors will fare no better in the long run than Commoner's reservations about sewage treatment if the technology progresses to the point of solving the problems.

An additional problem that bothered Commoner was the habit of looking at a problem in isolation and devising a solution that turned out to cause another problem, which required a new patch. The last chapter presents an example: industry responded to the mandate to eliminate fly ash emissions by building coal ash lagoons. Besides the ones that have made news by failing, all of them leak and pollute ground water. North Carolina recently enacted the first state law ever to control coal ash. State regulators and Duke Energy seem only to be looking for another convenient patch.

A newer approach to technological improvement is to look for ways to use problematic natural processes as a solution for other problems. For a small-scale example, a gardener had a problem with a rapidly growing pumpkin vine in a very small garden space. She also had a problem with squirrels invading the garden. As it turns out, squirrels dislike the prickly stems of pumpkin vines, so she trained the vine to grown around the perimeter of the garden. She gained flexibility in where to plant other vegetables, and the pumpkin vines deter the squirrels. Here are some technologically more sophisticated ways of using one problem to solve another (culled from various articles in my blog *Sustaining Our World):*

- British Airways and a partner are diverting organic waste from landfills to make it into jet fuel.
- New York City and Waste Management have initiated a procedure to process organic waste, and combine it with sewage sludge to produce biogas, which will cut the city's purchase of natural gas.
- Numerous pilot projects have demonstrated how to use manure to generate either electricity or usable biogas. A scientist at North Carolina A&T University has found a way to turn hog waste into a superior asphalt adhesive. Like manure to energy, manure to asphalt adhesive is a proven concept for making a valuable resource from a serous waste disposal problem.
- Waste plastic also makes an excellent aggregate for asphalt. Imagine driving on a highway made from recycled plastic and hog waste!
- At least two small companies are making waste plastic into new crude oil, and at least one is turning used motor oil into gasoline.
- Several fabric manufacturers are turning PET bottles (the plastic with the number 1 in the recycling symbol) into high-quality polyester fiber. Clothing made with it is available in stores now.
- German scientists have discovered how to use whey left over from cheese making into a biodegradable plastic to replace the films that protect cheese, meat, and other foods in grocery stores.
- Another German, both a microbiologist and fashion designer, invented a fabric (Qmilch) made from casein, another dairy waste and sells Qmilch clothing that she designs.
- Astronauts aboard the space shuttle found a way to make drinking water from urine with a forward osmosis process that requires no power source.
- At the summer Olympics in London (2012), sanitized sewer water provided not only water for flushing toilets and irrigating the landscaping, but even drinking water. Do not turn your nose up at drinking sanitized sewer water! If your drinking water comes from a river and there is wastewater treatment plant upstream, you're drinking and bathing in it now. The Olympic Delivery Authority turned to sewage when it became apparent that both groundwater and rainwater

would be too unreliable in quantity and too expensive to process.

— A British company called Knowaste has discovered how to make building materials from about the only wastes that seem more disgusting than sewage: dirty diapers and other absorbent hygiene products. The company also dries and gasifies the organic residue from the process to make green energy.

— TerraCycle, an American company, separates tobacco, paper, and filters from cigarette butts. It composts the organic products and makes building materials from the filters.

These and other imaginative uses of waste as a raw material have proved themselves technologically viable. They need only be scaled up for wider commercial application. Granted that sustainability faces technological, political, and social barriers, the greatest barrier to any of the small startup companies represented by the foregoing list is financial. Just about every industry segment has started as an entrepreneur's new idea. The entrepreneur needs money to turn the idea into a product and a company to sell it. Venture capitalists provide money and, in return, gain significant control over the new company's decisions. Venture capitalists risk their money with the expectation of getting a good return on it. Their interest, therefore, is to make small, struggling startups into companies large enough and well enough known to launch a successful initial public offering or other comparable financial success.

In other words, traditional venture capital is all about growing large companies and getting the quickest return on investment it can. Traditionally, that has resulted in concentration of industry after industry into a few large, centralized bureaucracies trying to use their capital as efficiently as possible. These in turn provide an abundance of standardized, relatively inexpensive products that rely on vast distribution networks. In example after example, efficient use of capital by large corporations requires inefficient, even wasteful use of natural resources. Economically and environmentally, this model is not sustainable. Venture capital as it is now practiced, does not know what to do with companies that plan to produce small-scale solutions to environmental problems designed to have a long-term impact.

For example, President George W. Bush, who warned the nation about its addiction to oil, championed biofuel from miscanthus, switchgrass and other non-food crops. So far, no one makes any such biofuel on a commercial scale. Miscanthus and switchgrass will grow on fields where the contents of manure lagoons have been sprayed without much need for maintenance. After all, a field sprayed with foul water from an animal waste lagoon has already been fertilized and irrigated. Laying aside remaining technological and political barriers to using these crops to make biofuel, once they have been harvested, they are far too heavy to transport very far. Therefore instead of a few large and centralized biofuel refineries, using these crops will require hundreds or thousands of small plants located within a few miles of the farms. That is a good thing for the environment. The new technology will not depend on long-distance shipping and all of the environmental consequences that causes. But how will start-up companies get seed money until someone comes up with a model for venture capital that will work on that scale?

The role of government

As Henry Ford II pointed out in 1970, industry cannot adopt environmentally responsible practices without government regulation setting standards. Despite the rhetoric of extremists like Tom DeLay, nothing has changed. The patchwork of conflicting state and local laws made everyone welcome the creation of the Environmental Protection Agency to work out some standard, nationwide policies. The AP-NORC poll described above shows that less than 60% of the public acknowledged that the federal government has a large amount of responsibility for increasing energy savings, and only 50% recognized any such role for state and local government. I have already described the development of federal environmental legislation and the rapid progress in improving the health of the environment after the EPA started to operate. I have no recommendation for improving the cooperation between federal and local governments as already described. It seems to work well.

The federal government is good at setting standards, but absolutely incompetent as a venture capitalist. For one example among too many, the Obama administration touted a solar company called Solyndra, which soon went bankrupt. It made a product marginally superior to other products on the market, but the cost of making it exceeded the price the market would pay for it. Most of its money, it appears, came from government grants. Certainly many environmental startup companies need some alternative to standard venture capital, but companies that fail to raise significant funding beyond government grants have little chance of success. This point is not a criticism of the Obama administration. The federal government wasted money on similar projects long before President Obama was born.

Many critics of wind energy complain that it can only work with hefty government subsidies. The coal industry, on the other hand, crows that it has subsidies and can therefore keep prices low. It would be good if the federal government would get out of the subsidy business entirely. Industries that win subsidies develop the lobbying power to keep receiving them long after the conditions that led to the subsidy in the first place have ceased to exist.

The federal government also makes agreements with foreign governments on a wide range of issues, including those that directly or indirectly affect the environment. At least since the Kyoto Protocol, adopted in 1997, the United Nations has attempted to deal with environmental issues using a centralized structure legally binding on all signatories. The United States is not a signatory. The Kyoto approach does not work. It cannot work. Someone noted in a forum discussion thread that technology can solve environmental problems only after human greed is taken out of the equation. Usually anyone who raises the issue of greed means specifically corporate greed, but it is certainly a mistake to stop there. One reason why the Kyoto Protocol failed is that it exposed the meeting grounds between the greed of established economies like the United States (both as a society and as individuals) and the greed of the rising economies like China.

Much of the world endorsed the Kyoto accords, but no nation has actually attempted to put them into practice. They would have meant economic ruin for rich countries. They allowed rising economic powers like China and India to pollute without any real restraint. They contained nothing to lift the world's poorest people out of abject poverty. None of the subsequent international meetings have produced anything any more workable. Nor can they. Most of the countries at the table know nothing about the social and political structures from which any of the truly imaginative solutions are likely to come. Even American and European governments are not likely to come up with policies that will foster sustainability if they conceive them from the top down. Earth Day 1970 demonstrated the possibility of important environmental policy changes initiated at the grassroots level.

Both the greatest human attainments and human abuses seem to come from centralization. The earliest man who enforced a claim to be king offered his people some protection against neighbors, but kings eventually sold their people on the notion that royalty was somehow a superior class of being. The United States should not forget the benefits of divided government, with both the federal and state governments dividing responsibility among three branches of government, in making any agreements within the international community.

State and local governments have a less recognized role in environmental law, but they are responsible for zoning, building codes, utility regulation, and so on. Every jurisdiction has its own building code. Each jurisdiction updates its code frequently. It may seem like building codes are a hodgepodge of the whims of local politicians. In fact, all local building codes must conform to state building codes. Most state building codes are modeled on the International Code Council (ICC). The ICC amounts to a merger in 1994 of three non-profit corporations that issued regional model building codes. It was founded on the belief that the U.S. should have only one set of model codes. The "international" in the name apparently comes from the fact that the federal government uses ICC codes for constructing facilities all over the world and that other nations use them as a reference.

The ICC, whose members represent the construction industry, has developed not one model code, but fifteen. Besides one simply called "International Building Code," there are codes for fire, plumbing, property maintenance, wildlife, urban interface, and more—even a green construction code. Each one of them touches on some building process that will directly affect the environment locally. Each model code is updated periodically, and each revision is more stringent than the last. Building codes are only one of several activities of state and local government that play a significant role in energy conservation. And yet half the American population does not recognize that that state and local governments have an important role in energy usage. I hope this book will motivate readers to see what else their states are doing.

I need not belabor the fact that all levels of government levy and collect taxes, and that changes in the tax code can change people's behavior in ways that are either favorable or unfavorable to sustainability.

Individuals beyond individual actions

Consideration of who has responsibility and power in this chapter began with the individual, and it will end there. It is not enough for individuals to take personal responsibility, but nothing else will happen if they do not. For example, environmental activists and industrialists need to speak *to* each other, not *at* each other. They must together consider the question of how to organize society and the economy so that they are sustainable environmentally, economically, and socially. And when they do, it will be individual people on both sides holding the conversations. Besides earlier recommendations of what sustainable choices people can make, only individuals

- Elect governments
- Run for office and serve if elected
- Go into business from single proprietorships to large industrial companies
- Work for businesses of all sizes and functions
- Teach at universities
- Study at universities
- Form and work for other non-profit organizations, including environmental watchdog groups.

The government is not some vast impersonal agency. It comprises the people who work for it, elected or otherwise. However well or badly the government plays its role, individuals and small groups of people ultimately make the decisions that, taken together, steer policies. Sustainability depends on a critical mass of these individuals being sensitive to environmental matters both as broad as passing laws and as narrow as saving energy and water in a particular workplace.

Corporations likewise are people. For all the scorn heaped on Mitt Romney for saying so, he was right in two different senses. That the Supreme Court has declared corporations legally persons is of no concern to this discussion. But a corporation is people from the CEO down the to the receptionist. New businesses get their character from the drive and vision of the individuals who founded them, which can include valuing or dismissing sustainability. They can grow into large corporations or not, but everyone who works at any level of a corporation has influence on other individuals in the workplace.

Teachers and academics have special influence in shaping the minds and behavior of students. Everyone who works for a government or corporation had teachers. The more teachers who both teach sustainability and live it out, the more likely it is that their students will live sustainably, whether the students are kindergartners or doctoral candidates. People studying or teaching disciplines that have nothing to do with sustainability are still individuals living out their values, still individuals whose disciplines do not limit their interest, still individuals whose words and actions influence people around them. Too many college and university professors teach what to think and not how to think. Too many college and university departments consciously seek demographic diversity among their faculty and then consciously or unconsciously avoid intellectual diversity by not hiring or denying tenure to people who think differently from everyone else. How is a department diverse if it can tick off impressive numbers of different demographics but has no centrists or conservatives? The most egregious anti-corporate claptrap seems to come from academics who cannot be bothered to learn anything about business or listen to other viewpoints carefully enough to recognize that people with different political views can still have genuine concern for the environment.

In 1970 there were four national conservation groups, and together they advocated for what seems now like narrow range of environmental interests. They had only begun to be politically militant. Their members came from across the political spectrum. Times have changed, and it is necessary to add one more bullet point to what only individuals can do:

- Keep an eye on environmental watchdog groups to induce them to live up to their stated goals.

As in 1970, the most vocal warnings of impending catastrophe come from the left wing, the virulently anti-corporate wing of American politics and academia. Trouble comes when their opposition to profit-making corporations trumps their concern for the environment. In the case of the Dan River coal ash spill, a leader of one environmental group criticized Duke Energy, and parenthetically the EPA, for halting the cleanup when only about 5% of the ash had been recovered. The Kingston cleanup recovered 95% of that spill. Why did Duke stop so soon? The comparison was calculated to make Duke look like a lazy and messy teenager. A few minutes of investigation and some basic arithmetic reveals that the amount coal ash that remains from the Kingston dam collapse after the cleanup was declared finished is 3,700 times what spilled into

Dan River in the first place. It is the author who looks more like a lazy teenager exerting minimal effort on a writing assignment.

Another group appeared to be more eager to give Duke a black eye than take care of the river. It threw incendiary prose up on its website so quickly that it did not even provide the correct date of the spill. It excoriated Duke's "arrogance" at announcing the end of the cleanup without acknowledging that, in fact, the EPA ordered the halt. It did not even mention the EPA in either of two posts. Neither group considered that since the Dan River was a dumping ground for industrial chemicals in an era before most people noticed or cared, the river bottom contained PCBs and other chemicals more toxic than coal ash. The environmental impact of releasing those substances back into the water would cause vastly more environmental harm than leaving scattered pockets of ash a few inches thick in the river. It is most unfortunate that some environmental watchdog groups would appear to care more about an evil corporation getting off the hook than the damage further cleanup would require.

Both government and industry get complacent. Both government and industry are likely to put a higher value on other things besides acting sustainably. It is good to have organizations dedicated to monitoring the decisions of government and industry to keep their feet to the fire when those decisions can cause harm or even irreparable damage to the environment. Someone needs to keep an eye on government and industry, and speak up, and we cannot afford to leave that mission entirely in the hands of organized lobbying groups. The general public ought to be equally wary of the environmental watchdog groups as any other special interest when the rhetoric becomes too intemperate.

A large portion of the American public does not believe that their individual choices matter. But they do matter. People in government, business, unions, academia, non-profits, or anyone else live in someone else's neighborhood. They shop and socialize and do what people in the neighborhood do. Does a green lifestyle seem normal in the neighborhood? Or is it weird? Achieving a sustainable society depends on a critical mass of people in all kinds of neighborhoods and from all walks of life believing that it is normal.

Bibliography

Alexander, Barbara T. "The US Homebuilding Industry: A Half-Century of Building the American Dream." John T. Dunlop Lecture, Harvard University, October 12, 2000

Allegre, Claude et al. "Concerned Scientists Reply on Global Warming." *Wall Street Journal*, February 12, 2012. http://online.wsj.com/article/SB10001424052970203646004577213244084429540.html?mod=WSJ_Opinion_LEADTop

Allegre, Claude et al. "No Need to Panic about Global Warming." *Wall Street Journal*, January 27, 2012. http://online.wsj.com/article/SB100014240529702043014045771715318384421366.html

Bennett, Graceann, and Freya Williams. *Mainstream Green: Moving Sustainability from Niche to Normal*. Ogilvie & Mather, 2011.

Blumberg, Louis, and Robert Gottlieb. *War on Waste*. Washington, DC: Island Press, 1989.

Boynton, Jen. "Jeffrey Hollender Shares Four Reasons He Got Fired from Seventh Generation." *Triple Pundit*. June 9, 2011. http://www.triplepundit.com/2011/06/jeffrey-hollender-seventh-generation-fired/

Brinkley, Douglas. "Rachel Carson and JFK, an Environmental Tag Team." *Audubon*. May-June 2012. http://www.audubon.org/magazine/may-june-2012/rachel-carson-and-jfk-environmental-tag-team

Brooks, Karl Boyd. *Before Earth Day: The Origins of American Envirnomental Law, 1945-1970*. Lawrence: University Press of Kansas, 2009.

Brown, Harrison. "Human Materials Production as a Process in the Biosphere." *Scientific American* (September 1970): 195-208.

Carter, Luther J. "Earth Day: a Fresh Way of Perceiving the Environment." *Science* (May 1, 1970): 558-59.

Carter, Luther J. "Environmental Teach-In: a New Round of Student Activism?" *Science* (January 16, 1970): 269.

Carter, Luther J. "Environmental Teach-In: University of Michigan Meeting Links Concerns about Pollution and 'Upside-Down Society'" Science (March 20, 1970): 1594-95.

Chen, Cindy, and Mike Hicks. "The Paradox of Politics." *Environmental Protection* (May 1, 2007) http://eponline.com/articles/2007/05/01/the-paradox-of-politics.aspx

Clebsch, Edward E. C. "The Campus Teach-In on the Environmental Crisis—1970." *Living Wilderness* 34 (Spring 1970): 10-12

Commoner, Barry. "Beyond the Teach-In." *Saturday Review* 53 (April 4, 1970): 50 ff.

Commoner, Barry. "Soil & Fresh Water: Damaged Global Fabric." *Environment* 12 (April 1970): 4-11

Cotton, Steve. "Earth Day—What Happened." *Audubon* (July 1970): 112-15.

Davis-Peccoud, Jenny, James Allen, and Melinda Artabane. "The Big Green Talent Machine." Bain & Company, April 17, 2013. http://www.bain.com/publications/articles/the-big-green-talent-machine.aspx

"Delay, Tom." Encyclopedia.com (2006) http://www.encyclopedia.com/topic/Tom_DeLay.aspx

"Earth Day: The History of A Movement." Earth Day Network Earth Day Expo, Habana Outpost, Brooklyn, April 19, 2008 http://www.earthday.org/earth-day-history-movement

Easterbrook, Gregg. "Forgotten Benefactor of Humanity." *The Atlantic*. January 1997. http://www.theatlantic.com/magazine/archive/1997/01/forgotten-benefactor-of-humanity/306101/

Easterbrook, Gregg. "The Man Who Defused the 'Population Bomb.'" *Wall Street Journal*. Updated September 16, 2009.

Ehrlich, Paul R. and Anne H. Ehrlich. "The Food-from-the-Sea Myth." *Saturday Review* (April 4, 1970): 53-55 ff.

Ehrlich, Paul R. and John P. Holdren. "The People Problem." *Saturday Review* (July 4, 1970): 42-43.

Ehrlich, Paul. "Ecological Destruction Is a Condition of American Life." *Madamoiselle* (April 1970): 188 ff.

Ehrlich, Paul. "People Pollution." *Audubon* 72 (May 1970): 4-9

Environmental Protection Agency. "EPA@40 40 Years of Achievements, 1970-2010: EPA@40." (2010) http://www.epa.gov/40th/achieve.html

Fotheringham, Alasdair. "World's Largest Solar Plant Powers Up." *The Independent*. January 1, 2012. http://www.independent.co.uk/environment/green-living/worlds-largest-solar-plant-powers-up-6283799.html

Gerlach, Luther P. "Eco-Gemini: Two for the Teach-In." *Natural History* 79 (May 1970): 71-75.

Gillis, Carly. "Santa Barbara Oil Spill: A Brief History." *Counterspill*. May 5, 2012. http://www.counterspill.org/article/santa-barbara-oil-spill-brief-history

Gofman, John W. and Arthur R. Tamplin "Radiation: the Invisible Casualties" *Environment* 12 (Spring 1970): 13-19 ff.

Griswold, Eliza. "How 'Silent Spring' Ignited the Environmental Movement." *New York Times Magazine*, September 21, 2012.

Guion, David M. *Sustaining Our World*. Blog: http://sustainingourworld.com

Guion, David M. *When the River Ran Gray*. Kindle e-book.

Gunter, Peter A. "Mental Inertia and Environmental Decay." *Living Wilderness* 34 (Spring 1970): 3-7

Haederle, Michael. "Solar Showdown: Are New Solar Power Projects Anti-Environmental?" *Pacific Standard* (April 18, 2011) http://webcache.googleusercontent.com/search?q=cache:http://www.psmag.com/books-and-culture/are-new-solar-power-projects-anti-environmental-29888

Hartman, Holly. "Milestones in Environmental Protection." *Infoplease*. http://www.infoplease.com/spot/earthdaytimeline.html

Hayes, Denis. "Environmental Teach In." *Living Wilderness* 34 (Spring 1970): 12-13

Hayes, Denis. "Earth Day." *Mother Earth News* 209 (Apr/May 2005): 24, 26-31.

Hedgpeth, Joel W. "The Oceans: World Sump" *Environment* 12 (Spring 1970): 40-47.

Humes, Edward. *Garbology: Our Dirty Love Affair with Trash*. New York: Avery, 2012.

"Killer Smog Claims Elderly Victims." *History.com* http://www.history.com/this-day-in-history/killer-smog-claims-elderly-victims

Lewis, Jack. "Looking Backward: A Historical Perspective on Environmental Regulations." *EPA Journal* (March 1988) http://www2.epa.gov/aboutepa/looking-backward-historical-perspective-environmental-regulations

"Main U.S. Environmental Laws." Carnegie-Melon University. http://environ.andrew.cmu.edu/m3/s7/us_laws.shtml

Main, Jeremy. "Conservationists at the Barricades" *Fortune* (February 1970): 144-47, 150-51

Miller, Henry I. "Norman Borlaug: The Genius Behind The Green Revolution." *Forbes* (January 18, 2012) http://www.forbes.com/sites/henrymiller/2012/01/18/norman-borlaug-the-genius-behind-the-green-revolution/

Natural Step. "The Four System Conditions of a Sustainable Society." (no date) http://www.naturalstep.org/en/the-system-conditions

Natural Step. "Understanding the Problem: [The Funnel and the Tree]" (no date) http://www.thenaturalstep.org/en/the-funnel

Nelson, Gaylord. "How the First Earth Day Came About." *Environlink.* http://earthday.envirolink.org/history.html

"Norman Borlaug—Facts." Nobel Prize web site .http://www.nobelprize.org/nobel_prizes/peace/laureates/1970/borlaug-facts.html

O'Donnell, Edward T. "The Great Cranberry Scare of 1959." *In the Past Lane.* (November 21, 2012) http://inthepastlane.com/2012/11/21/the-great-cranberry-scare-of-1959/

Packard, Vance. *The Waste Makers.* New York: David MacKay, 1960.

Perry, Mark J. "Today's New Homes Are 1,000 Square Feet Larger Than in 1973, and the Living Space Per Person Doubled over Last 40 Years." *American Enterprise Institute.* (March 26, 2014). https://www.aei.org/publication/todays-new-homes-are-1000-square-feet-larger-than-in-1973-and-the-living-space-per-person-has-doubled-over-last-40-years/

Peterson, Eugene K. "The Atmosphere: A Clouded Horizon." *Environment* 12 (Spring 1970): 32-39.

"Project Survival." *Environment* 12 (Spring 1970): 2-3.

"Recycling Facts & Statistics." *Keep America Beautiful* (©2013) http://www.kab.org/site/PageServer? pagename=recycling_facts_and_stats

Rome, Adam. "The Genius of Earth Day." *Environmental History* 15 (Apr 2010): 194-205.

Sato, Junichi, "No Longer a Target, Whales Are Collateral Damage." *New York Times.* January 10, 2013. http://www.nytimes.com/roomfordebate/2013/01/10/did-we-save-the-whales-19/overfishing-threatens-whales

Seldman, Neil. "Brief History of Post WW II US Recycling Movement." *Institute for Local Self-Reliance.* (June 6,2012) http://ilsr.org/history-post-ww-ii-recycling-movement/

Shepherd, Jack. "The Fight to Save America Starts Now" *Look* (April 21, 1970): 23-32.

Singh, Salil. "Norman Borlaug: A Billiion Lives Saved." *AgBioWorld.* http://www.agbioworld.org/biotech-info/topics/borlaug/special.html

Stromberg, Joseph. "Classical Gas: The Ancient Romans Were Pioneers of Air Pollution." *Smithsonian* (February 2013): 18.

Time. Issues from 1970.

Tomson, T. et al. "Energy Issues: How the Public Understands and Acts." The Associated Press-NORC Research Center for Public Affairs. (2012)

Van den Bosch, Robert. "Pesticides: Prescribing for the Ecosystem." *Environment* 12 (Spring 1970): 20-25

Wolfle, Dael. "After Earth Day." *Science* (May 8, 1970): 657

About the author

David M. Guion became interested in protecting the environment around the time of the very first Earth Day (1970). He served for three years on two different working groups of the Sustainability Committee at the University of North Carolina at Greensboro.

That experience introduced him to a much broader range of environmental issues and solutions than he had previously imagined. He started the blog Sustaining Our World (http://sustainingourworld.com) in 2010 to explore these exciting new ideas, one of his four blogs.

He worked as a music librarian at the university and has a doctorate in musicology. He has also taught adult Sunday school classes and Bible studies for 35 years. And so the other three blogs are Musicology for Everyone; Reading, Writing, Research; and Grace and Judgment.

His growing collection of ebooks includes When the River Ran Gray, about the 2014 coal ash spill on the Dan River. An excerpt begins on the next page.

Take a look at his Amazon author page for the rest of his books (http://www.amazon.com/David-M.-Guion/e/B003ZFJWWE).

If you enjoyed this book, please share it on social media and leave a review on Amazon.

Book excerpt.

When the River Ran Gray: the Dan River Coal Ash Spill in North Carolina, How Governments, Duke Energy, Environmentalists and the Public Failed, and Why Manmade Environmental Disasters Keep Happening. Chapter 1

Manmade environmental disasters run a distressingly predictable course. After an event makes the headlines—nationally or locally, depending on its scope—the finger pointing and acrimony begins. Investigation quickly uncovers warning signs that someone should have noticed much earlier. Or it finds slipshod workmanship that some inspector should have noticed.

The responsible corporation (if it does not declare bankruptcy) undertakes a cleanup, regulated and directed by state regulators and/or, for serious problems, the US Environmental Protection Agency (EPA). Eventually the cleanup concludes. More than likely, environmental groups voice dissatisfaction and complain that corporations always get off too lightly.

Along the way, news outlets and politicians muse about steps to take to make sure nothing of the kind happens again. New legislation and regulation may or may not be enacted.

Eventually the event disappears from the news. The eco-system recovers enough to look good to the untrained eye. Either some time later or at about the same time, in some other state, with some other industry, a manmade environmental disaster happens again.

On February 2, 2014 a coal ash retention pond owned by Duke Energy failed and spilled much of its contents into the Dan River near Eden, North Carolina. It was the third largest coal ash spill in American history. Even so, it remained mostly a local story. National news media took notice briefly and sporadically some time later.

The Dan River originates in Patrick County, Virginia and flows 214 miles into the Kerr Reservoir on the Roanoke River. The reservoir straddles the Virginia-North Carolina state line, and the Dan River crosses the border multiple times before finally entering the reservoir on the Virginia side.

It is a scenic river and a favorite spot for fishing, swimming, boating, canoeing, and other recreational activities. Besides activities in the water itself, visitors can enjoy numerous trails and scenic driving routes.

The Dan River also supplies drinking water for several towns and cities along its route, as well as water for farms. It is vital to the area as both an economic engine and for the health and wellbeing of people who live nearby.

Duke Energy's Dan River Steam Station was a state-of-the-art coal fired electric power plant when it was built in 1948. By 1955, it boasted three units with a combined net capacity of 276 kilowatts.

Duke added three natural gas turbines to the three coal turbines in 1968. By 2008, the technology at the Dan River Station had become obsolete. Duke announced plans to retire all six units. The company completed the process of closing the coal plants and retired them on April 1, 2008. The old gas units ceased to operate a few months later when the new 620-megawatt natural gas facility opened.

The required maintenance of coal plants, both active and retired includes dealing with the ash left over from burning the coal. There are two kinds of coal ash. Bottom ash either falls to the bottom of the furnace hopper or coats its sides. Fly ash escapes through the chimney. Formerly, it escaped into the atmosphere and polluted the air. Larger ash particles settled back to earth at a distance from the chimney that largely depended on wind speed. Fly ash contains more dangerous pollutants than bottom ash, but the two are mixed together for disposal.

Regulation of fly ash began in 1970 with the passage of the Clean Air Act and has become progressively more stringent since then. Companies with smokestacks stoutly resisted the requirement for scrubbers in smokestacks to deal with fly ash, but construction of ash ponds began long before any legal or regulatory requirement.

Duke Energy (then Duke Power) built its first one in the mid 1950s at its Riverbend plant. When that plant came online (October 29, 1929—the same day as the stock market crash at the start of the Great Depression), its workers lived in a nearby company town. At the end of World War II, demand for electricity surged, and electric companies began to build multiple new coal-fired generating plants. At about the same time, residents of Riverbend's company town began to complain about the soot that fell on it.

By the 1950s, many residents had moved out and Duke decided to close and demolish the village. But at about the same time, it also decided to add precipitators to the plant to coat the fly ash with water and make it sink back to the ground. It dug a hole, dumped the ash in it, and added enough more water to make a thick slurry that the wind could not disturb. It must have been one of the first coal ash ponds. Duke installed a pond or two at the Dan River plant at about the same time. (The site now has two ponds. It was the first that failed, and for the purposes of this book, it does not matter when the second was constructed.)

The Environmental Protection Agency does not consider coal ash a hazardous waste. Power companies can actually sell it to other industries as a raw material. For example, it can replace some of the Portland cement in concrete. But coal plants produce much more ash than they can recycle. Ash ponds became the method of choice for disposing of the 20% or so that the companies cannot sell.

The pond that failed had unique construction; it was the only ash pond ever built with drainage pipes running beneath it. The pipes were intended as a safety measure to keep storm water out of the ponds by conducting it directly to the river. Somehow, tunneling under the pond to install the pipe seemed like a good idea at the time. About 13 years ago, inspectors began to urge Duke Power to inspect the two pipes with video cameras. The company claimed that the pipes were made of reinforced concrete and that monthly inspection of the outflow would give advance warning of any potential problems.

A little more than a year after the spill, Duke Energy pled guilty to federal charges of negligence. The 42-page plea deal contains some details Duke did not publicly acknowledge any earlier. For example, some leaks were found as early as 1979. Personnel in Eden repeatedly requested video inspection of the pipes, but senior management always refused. The company claimed that the pipes were made of reinforced concrete and that monthly inspection of the outflow would give advance warning of any potential problems.

Actually, the first 800 feet were installed in the early 1950s, when corrugated metal pipe (CMP) was the industry standard. It kept its circular shape by means of structural fill compacted around it. CMP made very sturdy drainage culverts, but they had a crucial weakness. Over time, water and dirt penetrate the structural fill and begin to corrode steel, the principal material, especially at the joints between sections of pipe. As the pipe rusts, it loses its circular shape. Eventually it folds in upon itself and collapses. In 1968, the pipe was extended another 300 feet. By that time the construction industry had adopted reinforced concrete for tunneling underground.

The larger of two pipes ruptured on February 2, 2014 (Super Bowl Sunday), and coal ash began to flow through it into the river. Apparently a flattened four-foot section of CMP entered the adjacent intact pipe on the downhill side. As the contents of the unlined lagoon above began to enter the pipe, the pressure the sludge exerted expelled the fragment a thousand feet or so out of the other end of the pipe. Crews found a crumpled four-foot section of 48-inch CMP downstream in the Dan River on April 13.

Some 39,000 tons (130 cubic yards) of coal ash slurry spilled into the river. Someone at the plant noticed the spill at about 2:00 in the afternoon. Duke's environmental staff began to assemble at the plant about an hour later. At 5:00 Duke executive Davis Montgomery called emergency officials in Danville, Virginia, the first city downstream of the spill. The water department there had about three hours notice that a plume of coal ash was on the way.

After Stephen Johns, operator of the Danville water plant, received the warning, he began to pay special attention to turbidity (particles, usually dirt, that make water cloudy and may contain bacteria) and chlorine. As readings on the turbidity meter soared, Johns followed the standard procedure of adding more aluminum sulfate to the water to cause dirt particles to clump and become easier to settle out. It did not help, and he eventually stopped using that tactic.

Subsequent testing showed that while the raw water from the river and in the early stages of the treatment process showed high turbidity, the water that had undergone the entire process showed normal levels. The plant's filter beds were successfully screening the ash that had accumulated on top of them.

It appeared, therefore, that the town's water supply was clear and drinkable. Nonetheless, plant officials sought confirmation from an independent laboratory. Danville had a two-day supply of water treated before the spill, which gave the laboratory time to do its work. As it turned out, the ash actually increased the filters' efficiency.

The public, however, found little comfort in the finding that its drinking water was safe. Sales of bottled water soared, even though officials warned that it is not subject to the same stringent standards as municipal drinking water. A year later some residents still find their fear more persuasive than scientific fact and refuse to drink the city's water.

Duke's communication with Danville and the Danville plant's response to it are a textbook example of how to respond to a manmade environmental disaster. Its communication with the officials in North Carolina was such a comedy of errors that it is impossible to be sure what happened. Montgomery made some calls to Lance Metzler, County Manager of Rockingham County, where Eden is located, and Brad Corcoran, Eden's City Manager. Somehow he failed to convey any sense of urgency. When contacted by the *News & Record,* Metzler did not remember receiving a call. Corcoran took his call shortly before the second half kickoff of the Super Bowl. Since Montgomery said Duke was still investigating and promised to keep him informed, Corcoran did not consider that the problem demanded his immediate attention.

If either Montgomery, Metzler, or Corcoran had notified the county's emergency response personnel, they would have had opportunity to take action. As it was, they learned of the spill at lunchtime the next day. The time had passed when they could have put their skills and equipment to good use.

North Carolina's state emergency management center learned of the spill a few hours before Rockingham County emergency workers did, but 18 hours had elapsed since it started. Duke environmental specialist Allen Stowe notified dispatcher Jeff Childs, but like Montgomery did not communicate a sense of urgency. Did he fail to tell Childs specifically that coal ash had spilled, as opposed to simply wastewater? State officials place the blame squarely at his feet. They claim that if Stowe had given Childs an accurate and sufficient description of the problem, he would have notified officials in both the North Carolina Division of Water Quality and in Eden. In particular, they claim that Childs asked if the spill occurred in a source of drinking water and that Stowe answered, "Not in this location."

Duke, of course, disputes that narrative. Unfortunately, Childs took the call on a cell phone on the way back to his desk from the break room. He took no steps to request that Stowe call back on a landline so that the call could be properly recorded. He only wrote a description several days later. Both men tell the story to present their actions in the most positive light possible, but since no recording of the call exists, it will forever be impossible accurately to know what either man actually said.

The North Carolina Division of Emergency Management has since rewritten its rules to require that dispatchers report any call from a private company, regardless of whether they think the issue appears serious.

www.ingramcontent.com/pod-product-compliance
Lightning Source LLC
Chambersburg PA
CBHW070704290526
45790CB00001B/449